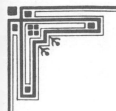
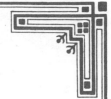

RURAL AMERICA
a Century ago

Edited by
S. H. Rosenberg

Printed 1976, 1979
ISBN: 0-916150-06-2

American Society of Agricultural Engineers
2950 Niles Road • P.O. Box 410
St. Joseph, Michigan 49085

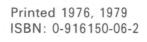

I

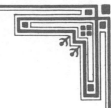
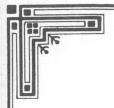

THE GROWTH

·•·OF·•·

INDUSTRIAL ART.

ARRANGED AND COMPILED UNDER THE SUPERVISION OF THE

HON. BENJ. BUTTERWORTH,

COMMISSIONER OF PATENTS AND REPRESENTATIVE OF THE DEPARTMENT OF THE INTERIOR OF THE UNITED STATES GOVERNMENT BOARD,

CINCINNATI INDUSTRIAL EXPOSITION, CINCINNATI, OHIO;

SOUTHERN EXPOSITION, LOUISVILLE, KENTUCKY;

THE WORLD'S INDUSTRIAL AND COTTON CENTENNIAL EXPOSITION, NEW ORLEANS, LOUISIANA.

Reproduced and Printed in Pursuance of Act of Congress, March 3, 1886, and Acts Supplementary thereto.

WASHINGTON:
GOVERNMENT PRINTING OFFICE
1892.

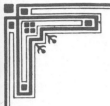
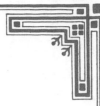

TABLE OF CONTENTS

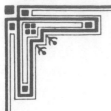

ABOUT THE SOCIETY

THE American Society of Agricultural Engineers (ASAE) is pleased to offer this historic work for those interested in the preservation of our American heritage.

The ASAE is a nonprofit engineering society which concentrates its efforts in service to agriculture. Currently, ASAE has some 8,000 members located primarily in the United States, and in some seventy other countries of the world. Its engineer-members concentrate their efforts in five major technical areas: (1) power and machinery, (2) soil and water, (3) structures and environment, (4) electric power and processing, and (5) food engineering. ASAE publishes a monthly magazine, *Agricultural Engineering,* which reports on present engineering developments and concepts. It also publishes research papers in *Transactions of the ASAE* and each year develops special publications on various subjects such as livestock waste management, field modification of tractors, dairy housing, compaction of agricultural soils, and so on.

ASAE also develops and publishes the voluntary standards which serve agriculture. These standards are published annually in *Agricultural Engineers Yearbook.* Included among the ASAE standards are those relating to power take-offs (specifications, terminology, speed), slow-moving vehicle emblem, moisture measurement (grain and seeds), and various standards relating to safety, uniform terminology, machine interchangeability, and the like.

ASAE works cooperatively with agricultural engineering departments in the various states, with the USDA and other branches of the federal government, and with engineers in private practice and those employed in industry, particularly the farm machinery industry. Through ASAE, these agricultural engineers work cooperatively toward further improvements in agricultural efficiency, productivity, and in the conservation and wise use of our soil and water resources.

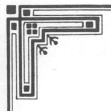

HOW THE FUTURE
OF AMERICA WAS INVENTED

IN this book are a few of the inventions that have moved the nation from pioneer life to a stage where millions may view on television a mechanical arm probing for signs of life on Mars. Where man's inventive genius may take us in the future no one knows.

Inventions and technology will continue to unfold the future for mankind. Primitive man gathered his food where he found it. Ages passed before the simplest of tools were devised. Then, with invention of the wheel mankind's future took a new turn. Civilization became possible. Man's existence became less precarious and his progress toward a better life proceeded in direct response to his inventive achievements. Today, progress is determined by inventive capability and enterprise. The stability and strength of governments and the standards of living of people are the products of invention.

It is interesting to study the relationship between invention and our own history. Page 12, reproduced from The Growth of Industrial Art, helps to illustrate this. Recorded here are patents relating to seeding machines. These are but a few of the thousands of inventions pertaining to farm machines made during this period.

Each series of inventions established a new step in agricultural production. Work output was increased, while the quality of work was improved and human drudgery eased.

By the turn of the century the inventions on these pages had enabled the Americans to develop the most efficient farms in the world. The incremental rate of crop production was sufficient to support a growing industrial system, and to export enough food and fiber to establish a favorable balance of trade with other nations. This input of technology has continued, and today farmers produce about six times as much per man-hour as they did fifty years ago.

America has always provided unique challenges for inventiveness. It became the home of people from many lands who came here to seek freedom and opportunity. Each undertook to apply skill and aptitude in a new world. The more venturesome and enterprising became prospectors, homesteaders, *inventors* and builders of American business.

Railroads opened up new frontiers. Electricity, telephones, automobiles, airplanes, and power farming ushered in continuous eras of growth, as did advances in chemistry, electronics, nuclear technology, computers, automation, and micro processing. The end is nowhere in sight as long as a favorable climate for inventiveness exists.

Today, we push buttons to wash and dry laundry. We have come a long, long way from the washing methods prevelent in 19th Century America. It has been this advancement in technology that has built the American enterprise system; creating jobs and enabling people to enjoy even more leisure time and greater prosperity. Inventiveness has built our cities and supported our institutions and government.

It is appropriate that the American Society of Agricultural Engineeers should publish this book. It portrays inventions, farm practices and modes of life in the 19th century when about 75 percent of the people lived in rural America. When agricultural engineering was established early in this century, it began by organizing and correlating a vast body of sciences and information pertaining to agriculture, crop production and processing, land resources, energy, power, machines, structures, ecology and countryside development into a distinct branch of engineering. Agricultural engineers have continued to extend technical services, counsel and influence to agriculture, industry and governments around the world.

G. B. Gunlogson
November 26, 1976

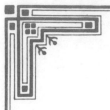

FOREWORD

I DON'T know if G. B. Gunlogson is the oldest living member of ASAE. Perhaps it's not that important anyway for being an "oldest living" member is a tenuous honor at best. Our records do indicate that G. B. Gunlogson, consulting engineer, became a member of this Society in 1913.

For a number of years now, the ASAE library has contained a volume entitled "The Growth of Industrial Art". The illustrations have always fascinated this editor. The copy has also been appealing in its quaint, archaic way. Until recently though, I never noticed the fine print at the very bottom of the title page, a modest line that reads: "Reproduced from original copy and published by G. B. Gunlogson, Mechanical Engineer, Product and Market Research, Chicago, Illinois." Somewhat to the right are the words, "Printed in U. S. A.—1935."

A few months ago, the Society received a letter from Gunlogson. He asked in an offhand manner if the Society would like the last six copies of the reprint still in his possession. Naturally, we said yes, we would.

The process that produced this book began with two questions. First, did anyone really care to view the 19th Century through the pens of patent office engravers? And secondly, was it worth our time and effort to edit a 200 page 15 in. x 19 in. book into a form that expressed Gunlogson's interest in preserving the original book: his lifelong devotion to improving the quality of life for rural America?

This book is an answer to the second question. The readers of this volume will determine its value as history; a history written a century ago.

Samuel H. Rosenberg
Editor
American Society of
Agricultural Engineers

PLOWS

T HE use of the plow can be traced to a very remote antiquity. "The Book of Job," the most ancient writing of The Old Testament, begins with an allusion to the plow.

The first idea of the plow was a crooked stick, of which various forms were used; then came the provision of an iron point. Up to this time the crooked sticks were on the principle of the double mold board, throwing off the earth on each side. The next step was to hew off one side of the sticks, so as to throw out the earth only on one side, approximating to a single mold board. Then the plow became a simple wedge, the land side being parallel with the line of the plow's motion, the other side moving the furrow still to the right, but leaving the furrow standing on edge. Then the wedge was gradually twisted so as to regularly invert the furrow.

Thomas Jefferson was one of the earliest American laborers in the effort to perfect and simplify the plow, his first ideas on the subject having been noted in his journal of 1788, although it was not until 1793 that he reduced his theory to practice.

The next American inventor was Charles Newbold, of Burlington County, New Jersey, who invented and constructed the

AGRICULTURAL IMPLEMENTS

1,943 Manufactories in the United States

	1860	1880
Capital Invested ...	$11,477,239.00	$62,109,668.00
Value of Productions, ...	17,599,960.00	68,640,486.00
Wages Paid, ...	5,080,549.00	15,359,610.00
Hands Employed ...	14,814	39,480

SUB CLASS
PLOWS

1,326,123 Manufactured in 1880

	Primitive Mode	Present Machines
CAPACITY—		
Acres per day, ...	1/2	20
Hands Employed per day	1	1

6,686 Patents Granted by the United States

first cast iron plow in America, for which letters patent were granted to him on June 28, 1797. After expending large sums of money in perfecting and introducing his invention, he abandoned the business in despair. The farmers conceived the idea that the "cast iron plow" poisoned the land, injured its fertility and promoted the growth of weeds.

The second patent granted by the United States for a plow, was to John Deaver, of Maryland, June 12, 1804.

Third, to D. Peacock, of New Jersey, April, 1807.

Fourth, to S. Vinton, of Connecticut, November 18, 1807.

Fifth, to H. Harris, of Kentucky, February 24, 1808.

Sixth, to R. B. Chenoweth, of Maryland, November 25, 1808.

Patents on plows were subsequently issued in the following order:

October 12, 1809, F. Woodward, New York.

October 12, 1809, U. & J. Nichols, New York.

July 13, 1810, S. Hall, Massachusetts.

August 10, 1811, J. Sanford, Connecticut.

September 7, 1812, J. Klay, Maryland.
February 8, 1813, J. Seeley, Maryland.
May 28, 1813, S. Tously, New York.
June 2, 1813, M. Patrick, New York.
August 7, 1813, M. Murray, Maryland.
August 28, 1813, H. Pease, Connecticut.

March 1, 1814, J. & J. Butler, Pennsylvania.

July 2, 1814, Jethro Wood, New York.
July 5, 1814, J. Swan, New York.
October 14, 1814, Morgan & Harris, New York.

November 9, 1814, Tously & Swan, New York.

December 17, 1814, H. Shultz, Pennsylvania.

October 13, 1816, J. Cromwell, Virginia.
May 29, 1817, D. Peacock, New Jersey.
July 31, 1817, J. Lupton, Virginia.
May 26, 1818, G. Davis, Maryland.
October 26, 1818, P. Miller, New York.
December 19, 1818, R. M. Harrison, New York.

December 28, 1818, G. D. Avery, New York.

Eleven of these patents were issued to citizens of New York, eight to Maryland, three

to Connecticut, two to Virginia, two to Pennsylvania, one to Kentucky, and one to New Jersey. After this time the inventors of plows multiplied so rapidly that only those are enumerated whose inventions involved new ideas, or such as have remarkably popular, viz: Harris, 1819; Burden 1819; Hingham, 1823; Hitchcock, 1823; Nourse, 1827; McCormick, 1831; Mears, 1831; Prouty, 1831; Jacobs, 1834; Webster, 1836; Webster, 1837; Witherow, 1839; Alger, 1839; Burrell, 1843; Holbrook, 1845; Mead, 1863.

Jefferson and Small discovered the importance of straight lines running from the sole to the top of the share and mold board; Pickering, the importance of a straight line running from the front to the rear; Jethro Wood, that all the lines running from the front to the rear should be straight; Knox, the method of laying down all the lines on a plane surface; Mears, the importance of a center draft, and the practical means of obtaining it by the inclination of the land inward.

Smith was the first to adopt two plows to work together, one of which threw two or three inches of the surface into the bottom of the preceding furrow, and the other covered it with the lower earth.

Gov. Holbrook invented a method by which plows of any size could be made symmetrical, either concave or convex, in such a way as to insure the complete pulverization of the soil.

It is strange, in view of the antiquity and importance of the plow, that its construction should have received so little attention from scientists, and that the principles of its construction should have been so little observed by those who used it.

There are, approximately, 900 establishments in the United States for the manufacture of plows, the annual product of which is estimated at $5,000,000.

The plowing of the land under cultivation in the United States is estimated at 180,000,000 acres, requiring the labor of 2,000,000 teams, either of oxen, horses or mules for 80 days each year.

1

PLOWS

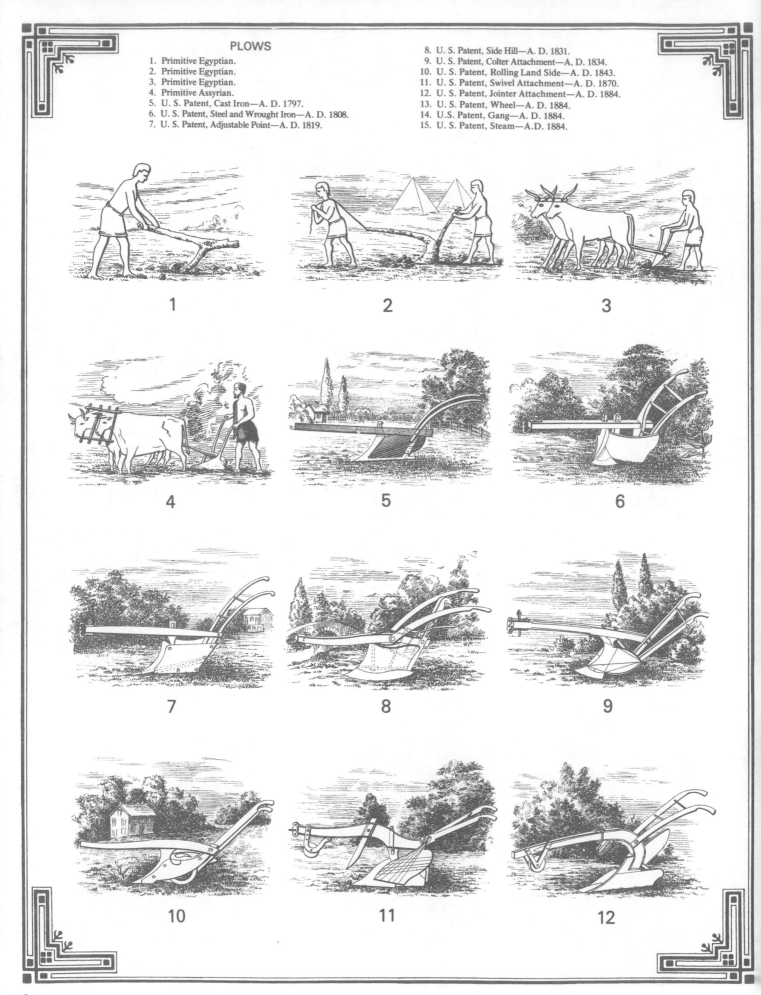

13

14

15

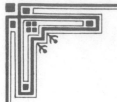

HARROWS

THE Harrow is mentioned three times in the Bible. First, in the book of Job, "Will he (the unicorn) harrow the valleys after thee." II Chronicles xx, 3, "He cut them with saws and with harrows of iron." In 2d Samuel, "He put them under saws and under harrows of iron."

The harrow was not in ordinary use in ancient Egypt. The various operations of husbandry at that period show that the clods of earch were either broken with hoes and plows, or by the trapping of men and animals.

Harrows bore the part in tilling the ground in the time of Pliny, A. D. 79, that they do at the present time: "after the seed is put into the ground, harrows with long teeth are drawn over it."

The harrow of the Romans was a hurdle. They also used planks studded with iron spikes.

There is a representation of a harrow in the tapestry of Bayeux, A. D. 1066.

One of the old modes of using the harrow in Ireland was to tie, with a cord of raw hide or bark, the trunk or brush limb of a tree to a horse's tail. This was abolished by act of Parliament, in the year 1664, "as being cruel and injurious to the animals."

In some parts of the north of Europe, the spiked limbs of fir trees are bound together. The spurs of the limbs make a reasonably fair substitute for the teeth of a harrow.

The usual form of the British harrow is called the "Berwickshire."

Double harrows are made in many forms, two, three or four leaved, having sections square lozenge shaped, trapezoidal, rhomboidal or triangular.

Rotary harrows are also made in various forms, and may have one, two or more sections, which lie flatly on the ground.

The spiked cylinder harrows are a late invention.

The spring harrow teeth, formed of spring metal, have been introduced, and are very extensively manufactured as a novel improvement in this line of inventions.

The concavo, convex and straight disk is one of the latest completed improvements.

Among the latest are those having inclined teeth set so, or set in bars susceptible of various inclinations.

HARROWS

1. Primitive Hand.
2. Primitive Log.
3. U. S. Patent, Rotary—A. D. 1859.
4. U. S. Patent, Rotary—A. D. 1859.
5. U. S. Patent, Disk—A. D. 1867.
6. U. S. Patent, Spring Tooth—A. D. 1869.
7. U. S. Patent, Wheel—A. D. 1876.
8. U. S. Patent, Disk—A. D. 1877.
9. U. S. Patent, Crushing—A. D. 1882.
10. U. S. Patent, Wheel Spring Tooth—A. D. 1884.

1

2

AGRICULTURAL IMPLEMENTS

1,943 Manufactories in the United States

	1860	1880
Capital Invested ...	$11,477,239.00	$62,109,668.00
Value of Productions, ...	17,599,960.00	68,640,486.00
Wages Paid, ...	5,080,549.00	15,359,610.00
Hands Employed ...	14,814	39,480

SUB CLASS
HARROWS

127,997 Manufactured in 1880

	Primitive Mode	Present Machine
CAPACITY—		
Acres per day, ...	1	30
Hands Employed per day.........	1	1

1,478 Patents Granted by the United States

3

4

5

6

7

8

9

10

CULTIVATORS

ANCIENT Roman writers recommended hoeing and weeding the corn and fallowing the ground.

The progenitor of the cultivating machine is the hoe. History furnishes no account of a time when man was distitute of the hoe and the plow; in the distant past they were all of wood; the original hoe was a forked limb.

The term "cultivator" embraces implements which are used in tending growing crops; it is an improved harrow.

Jethro Tull, of England, is the author of horse-hoeing husbandry, and introduced his system, in 1701, of cultivating plants by machinery. In 1731 he published a book on this subject which rendered the invention of the cultivator possible.

Wilkie, of Scotland, is the inventor of the cultivator. He invented in 1820, the plurality of shares, the expanding frame and the caster wheel.

The Finlayson cultivator was used in England in 1826.

Cultivators are direct off-shoots from the regular plow.

The first patent granted by the United States for cultivators was to Borden, in 1830.

The first wheel cultivator patent was issued in 1846.

The single shovel plow has been in use for many years; the double shovel is a later invention; it resembles some of the plows used for a thousand years or more in Asia and Southern Europe. The double shovel is nearly perfect for the purpose for which it is used, viz: that of tending a crop which is planted in hills, such as corn or potatoes.

The nearest approach to the American shovel plow is the Scotch horse hoe.

The Scotch grubber is a heavy cultivator, drawn by four horses and supported on wheels, for stirring and loosening the soil to plow depth.

Cultivators are classed in the United States as ordinary, wheeled, rotary, straddle-row, parallel, disk, walking, riding, vineyard and expanding.

CULTIVATORS

1. U. S. Patent, Wheel—A. D. 1846.
2. U. S. Patent, Rotary—A. D. 1858.
3. U. S. Patent, Straddle Row—A. D. 1869.
4. U. S. Patent, Wheel Parallel—A. D. 1879.
5. U.S. Patent, Disk—A. D. 1880.
6. U. S. Patent, Spring Attachment—A.D. 1883.
7. U. S. Patent, Spring Attachment—A.D. 1884.
8. U. S. Patent, Parallel, Riding—A. D. 1884.

1

2

3

AGRICULTURAL IMPLEMENTS

1,943 Manufactories in the United States

	1860	1880
Capital Invested ...	$11,477,239.00	$62,109,668.00
Value of Productions, ...	17,599,960.00	68,640,486.00
Wages Paid, ...	5,080,549.00	15,359,610.00
Hands Employed ...	14,814	39,480

SUB CLASS
CULTIVATORS

318,057 Manufactured in 1880

	Primitive Mode	Present Machine
CAPACITY— Acres per day	1	10
Hands Employed per day, ...	1	1

2,554 Patents Granted by the United States

4

5

6

7

8

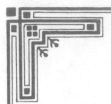

CULTIVATORS—WALKING

THE walking cultivator is of modern invention, and is one in which the operator walks behind, as distinguished from the riding cultivator.

Many American cultivators are constructed with triangular or rectangular frames, with handles like those of a plow, with a greater or less number of teeth, and with their center beams projecting in front for the attachment of wheels and draft clevises.

They are very extensively manufactured and used in the United States, and are frequently called "horse hoes."

1

AGRICULTURAL IMPLEMENTS

1,943 Manufactories in the United States

	1860	1880
Capital Invested ...	$11,477,239.00	$62,109,668.00
Value of Productions, ...	17,599,960.00	68,640,486.00
Wages Paid, ...	5,080,549.00	15,359,610.00
Hands Employed ...	14,814	39,480

2

SUB CLASS
CULTIVATORS—WALKING
318,057 Manufactured in 1880

	Primitive Mode	Present Machine
CAPACITY— Acres per day,	1	10
Hands Employed per day, ...	1	1

772 Patents Granted by the United States

3

CULTIVATORS—WALKING

1. Primitive Crotched Stick.
2. Primitive Egyptian.
3. Primitive Roman.
4. Primitive English.
5. U. S. Patent, Hilling—A. D. 1830.
6. U. S. Patent, Straddle Row—A. D. 1835.
7. U. S. Patent, Hilling—A. D. 1837.
8. U. S. Patent, Parallel—A. D. 1851.
9. U. S. Patent, Parallel Runner—A. D. 1884.
10. U. S. Patent, Straddle Row—A. D. 1884.

4

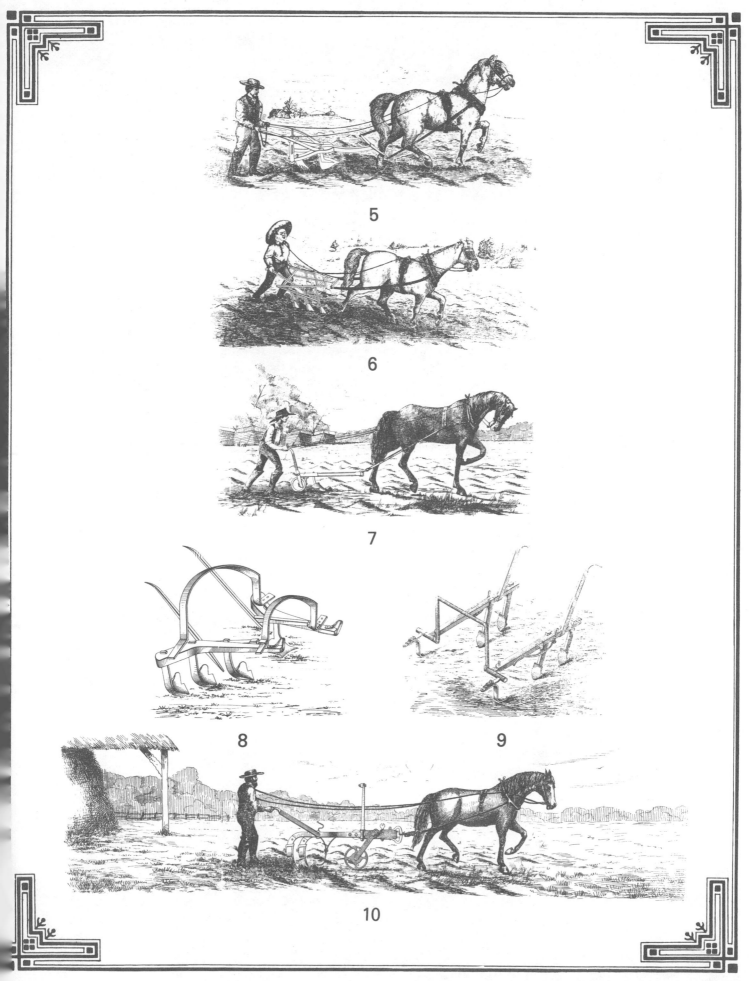

5

6

7

8

9

10

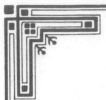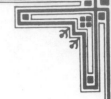

PLANTERS

PLINY says the Romans sowed their corn with as much care as they raised their armies.

Columbus found the natives of the West Indies using bread of maize.

Humboldt says that the cultivation of maize was introduced into Mexico in 666 by the Toltecs.

When Capt. John Smith visited Virginia in 1609, in writing of the Indians, he says: "The greatest labor they take is in planting corn."

About 1649 Gabriel Platte described a dibbling machine, formed of iron pins "made to play up and down like virginal jacks."

The Jesuit Lana, about the year 1665, proposed a planting machine to consist of a harrow, the spikes of which should make holes in the earth and the grains of corn were to fall from a box pierced like a sieve and placed over the harrow.

One of the first patents granted by the United States for a corn planter was a box that was placed on the shank of a hoe.

Planters are classified in the U. S. Patent Office as follows:

Corn, Cotton, Foot, Hand, Hand Oscillating, Hand Reciprocating, Hand Rotating, Potato, Potato Walking, Walking, Walking Vibrating Hoppers.

In the States which produce the greatest quantity of corn the larger part is planted by machinery.

PLANTERS

1. Primitive Hand.
2. Primitive Dibbler.
3. Primitive Dibbler.
4. Modern Hand.
5. U. S. Patent Wheelbarrow—A. D. 1825.
6. U. S. Patent Hand—A. D. 1856.
7. U. S. Patent Foot—A. D. 1856.
8. U. S. Patent Hand—A. D. 1876.
9. U. S. Patent Cotton—A. D. 1876.
10. U. S. Patent Cotton—A. D. 1883.
11. U. S. Patent Check Row—A. D. 1883.

1

2

3

AGRICULTURAL IMPLEMENTS

1,943 Manufactories in the United States

	1860	1880
Capital Invested ...	$11,477,239.00	$62,109,668.00
Value of Productions, ...	17,599,960.00	68,640,486.00
Wages Paid, ...	5,080,549.00	15,359,610.00
Hands Employed ...	14,814	39,480

SUB CLASS
PLANTERS

87,979 Machines Manufactured in 1880

	Primitive Mode	Present Machine
CAPACITY—		
Acres per day, ...	2	12
Hands Employed per day.........	1	1

2,497 Patents Granted by the United States

4

5

6

7

8

9

10

11

SEEDERS

SEEDING in ancient Egypt was done by scattering the seed upon the mud left after the receding waters of the Nile. The husbandman who scattered it was followed by a flock of sheep or goats, whose feet trod the seed into the surface of the soil.

The first seeding machine is said to have been used by the Assyrians, 504 B. C., and was called a drill plow.

The Italians claim the honor of originating, in 1605, the first seeder.

In the year 1623, Alexander Hamilton, of England, was granted a license for his protection in developing his invention of a seeding machine.

In 1634, David Ramsey made an attempt in the same direction, but without success.

Joseph Locatelli, of Austria, was the next to enter the field with a seeder. The exact date of the invention cannot be determined, but there is evidence that a trial of the machine took place at Luxembourg, in 1662. He obtained a patent for it in Spain. It was held in such high esteem that the Earl of Sandwich sent it to England.

In 1730, the attention of Jethro Tull, the inventor of horse-hoeing, was called to this machine, who was delighted with its adaptability to his mode of cultivation.

The first patent granted by the United States for a seeder was to E. Spooner, of Vermont, January 25, 1799. Hornsby, of England, was the first to apply india rubber tubes as grain spouts, in place of tin cups.

The American grain drill is usually drawn by a pair of horses, and has a gang of shares, in one or two banks. Some varieties have a capacity for changing to a single or double bank drill.

SEEDERS

1. Primitive Egyptian.
2. Primitive Assyrian—B. C. 504.
3. Primitive Italian—A. D. 1605.
4. U. S. Patent, Slide Broadcast—A. D. 1835.
5. U. S. Patent, Rotary Broadcast—A. D. 1856.
6. U. S. Patent, Broadcast Cultivator Attachment— A. D. 1869.
7. U. S. Patent, Grain Drill—A. D. 1874.
8. U. S. Patent, Broadcast Harrow Attachment— A. D. 1878.
9. U. S. Patent, Walking Drill—A. D. 1881.
10. U. S. Patent, Grain Drill—A. D. 1884.
11. U. S. Patent, Grain Drill—A. D. 1884.

1

2

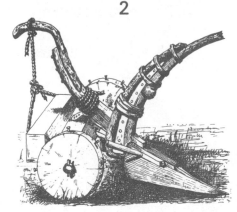

3

4

AGRICULTURAL IMPLEMENTS
1,943 Manufactories in the United States

	1860	1880
Capital Invested ...	$11,477,239.00	$62,109,668.00
Value of Productions, ...	17,599,960.00	68,640,486.00
Wages Paid, ...	5,080,549.00	15,359,610.00
Hands Employed ...	14,814	39,480

SUB CLASS
SEEDERS
79,074 Manufactured in 1880

	Primitive Mode	Present Machine
CAPACITY— Acres per day, ...	3 to 5	10 to 20
Hands Employed per day, ...	1	1

1,440 Patents Granted by the United States

5

6

7

8

9

10

11

DIGGERS

THE spade as a digging instrument does not seem to have been known in Ancient Egypt; its place was supplied by a heavy hoe.

The Ancient Greek spade has two cross pieces for the foot.

The Irish spade has a single cross piece for use with the right foot.

Many attempts to devise a machine which shall plow up potatoes from the furrow, separate them from the loose earth and deposit them on the surface of the ground, have been made.

The modern potato digger is a machine drawn by horses, which digs the potatoes, separates them from the dirt, and loads them into a cart, whilst the farmer rides on the machine with nothing to do but guide his team.

Diggers operated by steam take out 800 barrels of potatoes per day.

AGRICULTURAL IMPLEMENTS

1,943 Manufactories in the United States

	1860	1880
Capital Invested ...	$11,477,239.00	$62,109,668.00
Value of Productions, ...	17,599,960.00	68,640,486.00
Wages Paid, ...	5,080,549.00	15,359,610.00
Hands Employed ...	14,814	39,480

SUB CLASS
DIGGERS

33,453 Potato Diggers Manufactured in 1880

	Primitive Mode	Present Machine
CAPACITY—		
Acres per day, ...	1/2	10
Hands Employed per day, ...	1	1

952 Patents Granted by the United States

DIGGERS

1. Primitive Hand.
2. Primitive Egyptian Hoe.
3. Primitive Chinese Spade.
4. U. S. Patent, Hand Potato Digger—A. D. 1856.
5. U. S. Patent, Digging Hoe—A. D. 1871.
6. U. S. Patent, Separating Digger—A. D. 1876.
7. U. S. Patent, Vibrating Digger—A. D. 1882.
8. U. S. Patent, Rotary Digger—A. D. 1882.

1

2

3

4

5

6

7

8

9

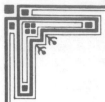

BEAN AND CLOVER HARVESTERS

THERE are several forms of bean harvesters:

1. The hand puller, having a long row of teeth to catch, and a movable clamp which comes down upon the teeth to grip, the vines.

2. A machine with a broad, flat, oblique share, which cuts the roots beneath the surface, followed by lifting bars which raise, and a rake which collects, the vines in a bunch. By oscillating the rake the bunch is dumped upon the ground.

3. A plow, which cuts the vines below the surface, and lifting and directing rods, which conduct them to a box on the machine.

4. A machine with a pair of horizontal toothed wheels rotating in apposition, so as to grasp the vines at the ground surface, and lift them so that they may be grasped by a traveling elevator belt, which deposits them in a box of the machine.

5. A wheeled machine, in which the pulleys are guided in and out of a hollow cylinder by a cam guide, so as to catch the haulm, lift it and carry it upward and over, and then, by retroaction of the puller arms, leave the vines upon the platform. The pullers rest upon springs, and are projected by the same in the interval of their retraction by the cam guide.

Clover harvesters are constructed on the same principle as the wheat harvester of ancient Gaul. In this machine it was the duty of the attendant to sweep the ears of grain back into the box of the machine, which was driven before the ox that impelled it.

The English clover harvester of thirty years back was of the Gallic pattern, and was drawn by one horse and guided by handles in the rear. The load was scraped out occasionally, and deposited in bunches in the field.

BEAN AND CLOVER HARVESTERS

1. U. S. Patent, Clover—A. D. 1849.
2. U. S. Patent, Clover Stripping Drum—A. D. 1854.
3. U. S. Patent, Clover Head Cutter and Breaker—A. D. 1856.
4. U. S. Patent, Bean Stalk Cutter and Bundler—A. D. 1859.
5. U. S. Patent, Clover Spiral Drum—A. D. 1861.
6. U. S. Patent, Bean Underground Cutter—A. D. 1865.
7. U. S. Patent, Clover Head Stripper—A. D. 1877.
8. U. S. Patent, Bean Stalk Puller—A. D. 1879.

AGRICULTURAL IMPLEMENTS
1,943 Manufactories in the United States

	1860	1880
Capital Invested ...	$11,477,239.00	$62,109,668.00
Value of Productions, ...	17,599,960.00	68,640,486.00
Wages Paid, ...	5,080,549.00	15,359,610.00
Hands Employed ...	14,814	39,480

SUB CLASS
BEAN HARVESTERS

	Primitive Mode	Present Machine
CAPACITY—		
Acres per day,....	1 1/2	10
Hands Employed per day, ...	1	1

22 Patents Granted by the Unites States

SUB CLASS
CLOVER HARVESTERS

	Primitive Mode	Present Machine
CAPACITY—		
Acres per day,....	1 1/2	20
Hands Employed per day, ...	1	1

44 Patents Granted by the United States

1

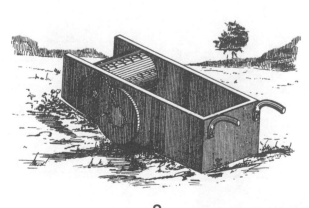

2

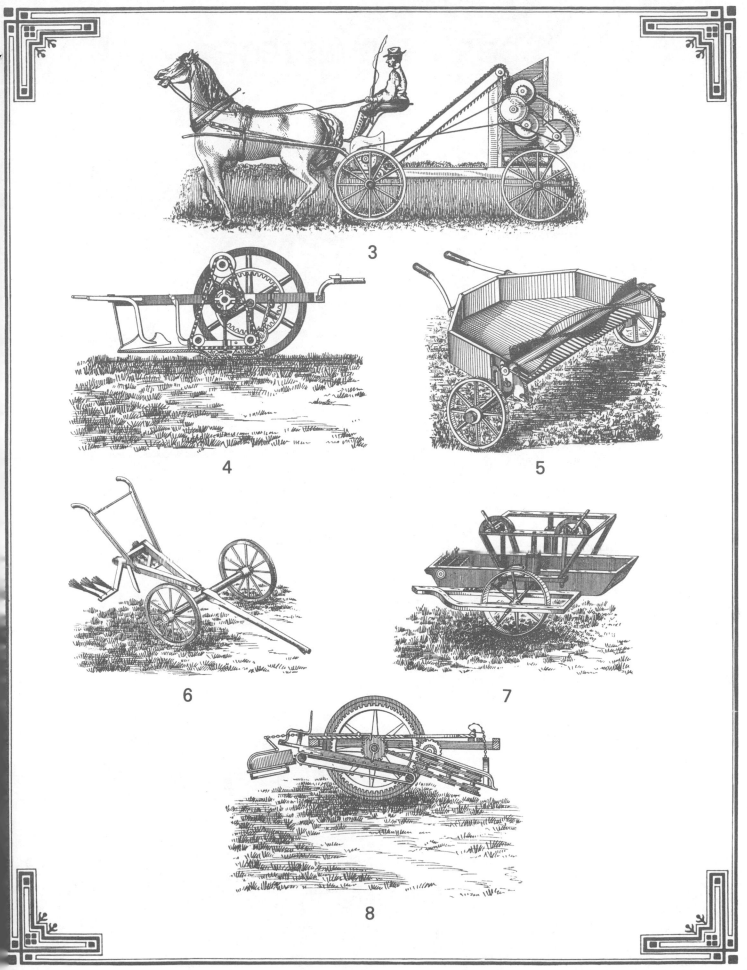

3

4

5

6

7

8

CORN HARVESTERS

THE Romans cut their corn by hand, either close to the ground, with a hook, or only the ears, with a curved stick having a saw attached to it, or they cut the stalks in the middle, leaving the stubble to be afterwards mowed.

The modern corn harvester is a machine for cutting corn in the field; sometimes delivering the corn in shocks, sometimes merely laying it in gavels upon the ground, or on the machine, whence it is taken by hand and shocked.

1

AGRICULTURAL IMPLEMENTS
1,943 Manufactories in the United States

	1860	1880
Capital Invested ...	$11,477,239.00	$62,109,668.00
Value of Productions, ...	17,599,960.00	68,640,486.00
Wages Paid, ...	5,080,549.00	15,359,610.00
Hands Employed ...	14,814	39,480

SUB CLASS
CORN HARVESTERS

	Primitive Mode	Present Machine
CAPACITY—		
Acres per day, ...	1 1/2	10
Hands Employed per day, ...	1	1

286 Patents Granted by the United States

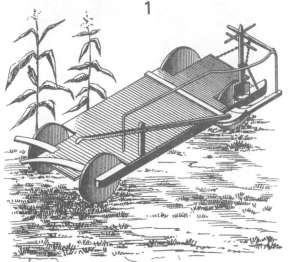

2

CORN HARVESTERS

1. Primitive.
2. U. S. Patent, Cutter—A. D. 1844.
3. U. S. Patent, Ear Stripper—A. D. 1850.
4. U. S. Patent, Ear Stripper, Husker and Sheller—A. D. 1850.
5. U. S. Patent, Cutter and Shocker—A. D. 1852.
6. U. S. Patent, Cutter and Shocker—A. D. 1854.
7. U. S. Patent, Cutter and Shocker—A. D. 1856.
8. U. S. Patent, High and Low Cutter—A. D. 1859.
9. U. S. Patent, Cutter and Shocker—A. D. 1866.
10. U. S. Patent, Picker and Husker—A. D. 1867.
11. U. S. Patent, Picker, Husker and Shocker—A. D. 1869.
12. U. S. Patent, Cutter, Husker and Shocker—A. D. 1875.

3

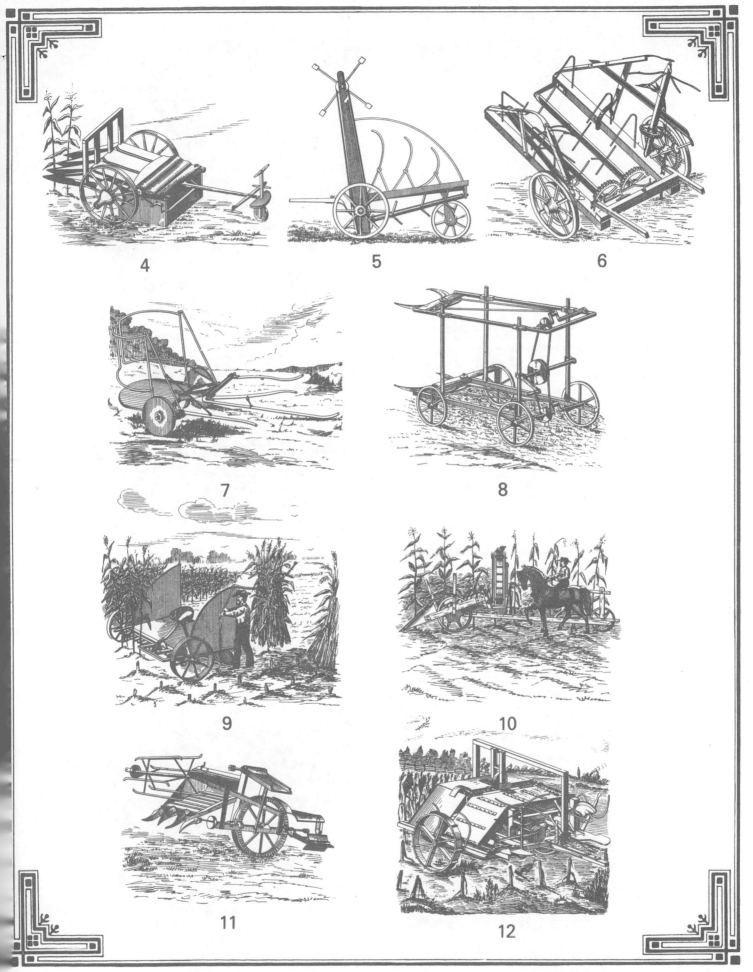

4

5

6

7

8

9

10

11

12

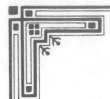

COTTON HARVESTERS

THE season for harvesting cotton in the United States begins in August, and continues until November, and sometimes even until the latter part of December.

The cotton plant continues to produce and ripen its bolls until the appearance of frost. The height of the picking season is in October.

Harvesting by hand is generally performed by negroes, both male and female, who, with widemouthed sacks suspended from their waists, pass between the rows of plants and gather the fleecy cotton from the open pods, when it is carried in the sacks and deposited in baskets at the end of the rows; the average amount per person picked per day being from 200 to 300 pounds.

The primitive mode of harvesting is the most general.

AGRICULTURAL IMPLEMENTS

1,943 Manufactories in the United States

	1860	1880
Capital Invested . . .	$11,477,239.00	$62,109,668.00
Value of Productions, ...	17,599,960.00	68,640,486.00
Wages Paid, ...	5,080,549.00	15,359,610.00
Hands Employed . . .	14,814	39,480

SUB CLASS

COTTON HARVESTERS

	Picked by Primitive Mode	Gathered by Present Machine
CAPACITY— Acres per day,		
Pounds per day, . .	300	1,500
Hands Employed per day	1	1

104 Patents Granted by the United States

COTTON HARVESTERS

1. Primitive Hand.
2. U. S. Patent, Toothed Picking Disks & Cylinders—A. D. 1850.
3. U. S. Patent, Hand Picker—A. D. 1855.
4. U. S. Patent, Brush Stripper—A. D. 1859.
5. U. S. Patent, Exhaust Flexible Pipe—A. D. 1859.
6. U. S. Patent, Fan Blower—A. D. 1868.
7. U. S. Patent, Saw and Stripper Brush—A. D. 1870.
8. U. S. Patent, Electric Belt—A. D. 1870.
9. U. S. Patent, Picker Stem—A. D. 1872.
10. U. S. Patent, Toothed Cylinder—A. D. 1874.
11. U. S. Patent, Revolving Picker Stems—A. D. 1878.
12. U. S. Patent, Toothed Cylinder—A. D. 1883.

1

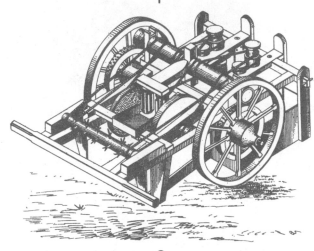

2

3

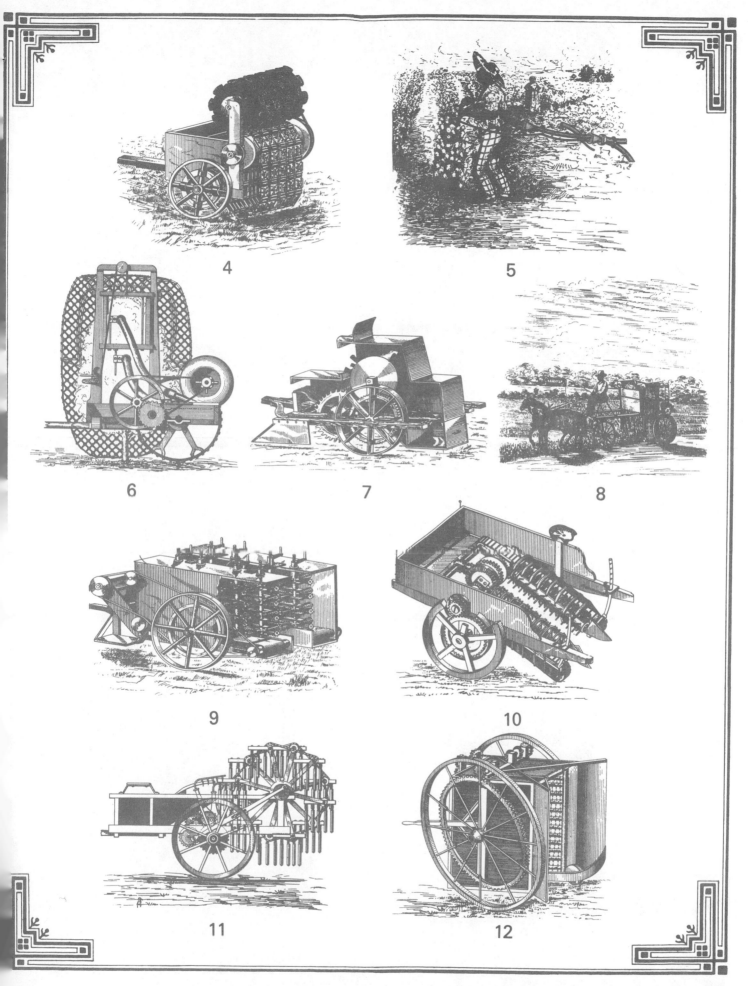

4

5

6

7

8

9

10

11

12

HEMP AND FLAX HARVESTERS

HEMP and flax harvesters are reaping machines resembling those for corn in their adaptation to operate upon tall top-heavy stalks, and differ from them in cutting low. One form is a puller, which grasps the stalks near the ground and uproots them. Another variety is one with a low platform on wheels, with a cutter bar in front, a reel to gather the stalks to the knives and direct them over into a cradle where they are collected in a bunch. In another form the stalks are caught by an arm till a shock is collected.

The stalk puller consists of a pair of revolving disks on axes, set at an obtuse angle with each other, so as to grip the stalks, which are conducted between them at the lowest part of their revolution, and then open as they rotate, and allow the stalks to fall into a cradle on the ground.

AGRICULTURAL IMPLEMENTS

1,943 Manufactories in the United States

	1860	1880
Capital Invested ...	$11,477,239.00	$62,109,668.00
Value of Productions, ...	17,599,960.00	68,640,486.00
Wages Paid, ...	5,080,549.00	15,359,610.00
Hands Employed ...	14,814	39,480

SUB CLASS
HEMP AND FLAX HARVESTERS

	Primitive Mode	Present Machine
CAPACITY—		
Acres per day, ...	1 1/2	10
Hands Employed per day	1	1

36 Patents Granted by the United States

HEMP AND FLAX HARVESTERS

1. U. S. Patent, Revolving Pulling Drum & Band— A. D. 1838.
2. U. S. Patent, Revolving Pulling Roller—A. D. 1852.
3. U. S. Patent, Reciprocating Pulling Jaw—A. D. 1863.
4. U. S. Patent, Stalk Plant—A. D. 1866.
5. U. S. Patent, Side Delivery—A. D. 1870.
6. U. S. Patent, Side Delivery—A. D. 1871.
7. U. S. Patent, Stalk Cutter—A. D. 1872.

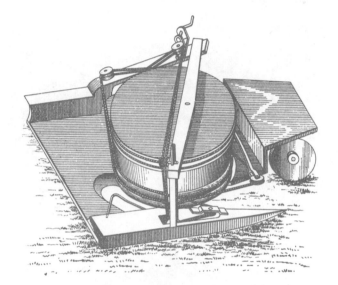

1

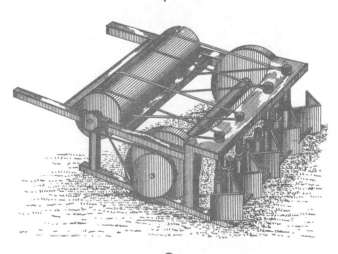

2

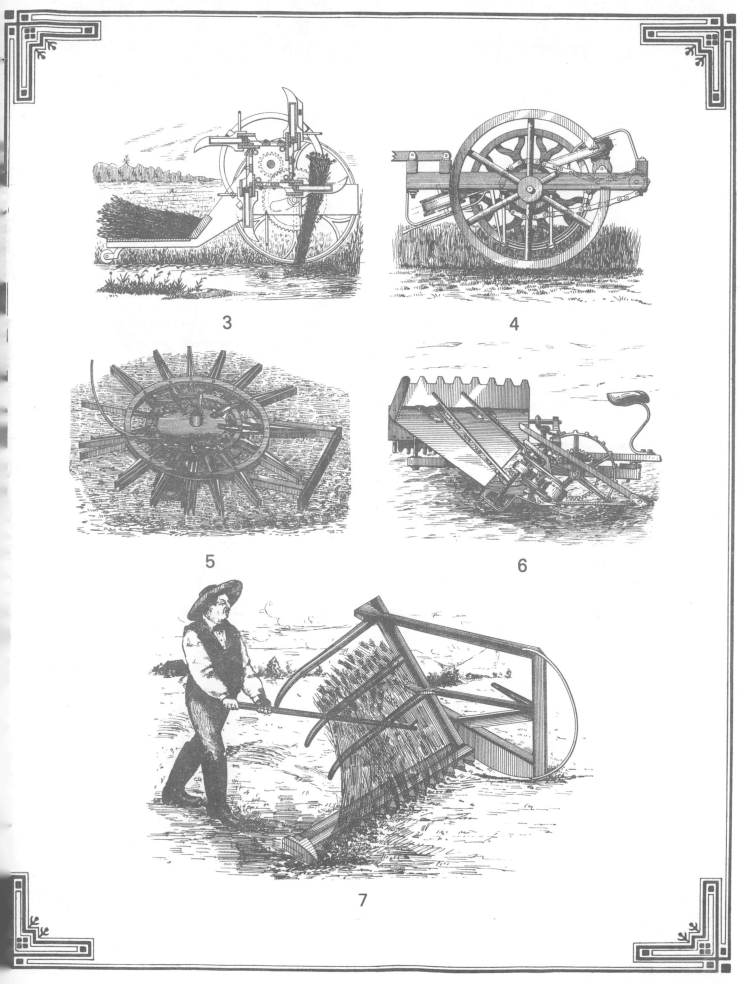

3

4

5

6

7

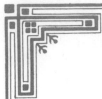

HARVESTER CUTTING APPARATUS

FAR back in the history of art "Time" himself is represented as a winged old man with a primitive scythe in his hand.

A charming harvest scene is presented to us in the Bible, when the loyal-hearted Ruth bends above the golden sheaves cut down by the scythes of the laborers of Boaz. This scene has been the theme of song and story since the time that the chivalrous son of Judah lifted the beautiful daughter of Moab, from among the humble gleaners in the field, to be the mistress of his heart and home. It has been reproduced in stained glass in our church windows, painted on the artist's canvas, and retained in the picture gallery of the mind by every one who ever read the pathetic narrative told in the brief Book of Ruth.

The scythe of the present day is of Anglo-Saxon origin, and was first spelled "sithe."

In ancient days a scythe was affixed to the axles of war chariots, intended, like that held by "Time," to mow down men instead of grain.

With the advancement of civilization, however, this useful apparatus became associated solely with the peaceful implements of agriculture, and has even furnished a convenient rhyme for the poets in their pastoral songs and gentler epics.

AGRICULTURAL IMPLEMENTS

1,943 Manufactories in the United States

	1860	1880
Capital Invested ...	$11,477,239.00	$62,109,668.00
Value of Productions, ...	17,599,960.00	68,640,486.00
Wages Paid, ...	5,080,549.00	15,359,610.00
Hands Employed ...	14,814	39,480

SUB CLASS
HARVESTER CUTTERS AND MOWERS

72,090 Manufactured in 1880

	Primitive Mode	Present Machine
CAPACITY—		
Acres per day, ...	1 1/2	30
Hands Employed per day........	1	1

1,610 Patents Granted by the United States

For instance, even Puritan John Milton sings:

"While the milkmaid singeth blythe
  And the mower whets his scythe."

Man has hammered at the problem of finding the most convenient and available machine for harvesting for centuries.

The harvester used in the plains of Rhætia, in the time of Pliny, had no proper motion, but was simply a comb whose teeth had sharp edges which tore and cut the head of the grain from the stalk and allowed it to be brushed into the box of the machine.

A harvest scene of ancient Egypt is shown by an illustration found in a tomb at Thebes, 1490 B. C. The reaper here uses the scythe, which has precedence of every other harvesting machine. The grain seems to have been cut at this time just below the ear.

Other methods of harvesting were practiced in Gaul in the time of Pliny. One was to pull the grain up by the roots, bind it in bunches, and then each bunch was drawn over a comb or hackle. This manner of harvesting is represented in a tomb at Eilethyas.

The Greeks and Romans used the curved sickle of the Egyptians, with but slight alterations. Varro describes three modes of reaping as common in Italy:

1. Cut low by a hook, the ears being afterwards cut off and sent to the granary.

2. Cut off below the head by a toothed sickle, and the heads carried off in baskets.

3. Cut off at half the length of the straw.

From the primitive curved blade of our Anglo-Saxon forefathers many improvements have been made. Modern invention now lays low in the short space of an hour vast fields of ripened grain. No longer is it necessary to bend over the scythe, but a machine propelled by horse-power or steam fells at a swoop the myriads of stalks whose crests are heavy with the seed of wheat, oats, hay, etc.

Later inventions are propelled by steam instead of horse-power. The apparatus consists of a boiler and steam engine, erected on a light wrought-iron girder frame, the whole being carried on four wheels, of which the two hind wheels are utilized for propulsion and the two fore wheels for steerage and for carrying

the cutting apparatus free of the ground. This powerful machine is used almost exclusively on the great wheat fields of the West and Northwest.

HARVESTER CUTTING APPARATUS

1. Primitive Grass Hook.
2. U. S. Patent, Reciprocating Serrated Cutter—A. D. 1881.
3. U. S. Patent, 2 Cutters Reciprocating in Opposite Directions—A. D. 1850.
4. U. S. Patent, Endless Chain Cutter—A. D. 1855.
5. U. S. Patent, Wave Wheel Reciprocating Cutter—A.D. 1855.
6. U. S. Patent, Rotary Cutters—A. D. 1856.
7. U. S. Patent, Vibrating Cutters—A. D. 1856.
8. U. S. Patent, Spiral Cutters—A. D. 1857.
9. U. S. Patent, Differential Gear Gyrating Motion—A. D. 1870.

1

2

3

4

5

6

7

8

9

LAWN MOWERS

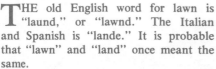

THE old English word for lawn is "laund," or "lawnd." The Italian and Spanish is "lande." It is probable that "lawn" and "land" once meant the same.

John Evelyn, a wealthy gentleman of the court of Charles II, devoted much of his leisure and money to pastoral pursuits. He is, perhaps, the first author who wrote of mowing "carpet walks."

Evelyn was one of the founders of what is known as "English landscape gardening." He was born in 1620, and wrote two able books, "Silva" and "Terra", bearing upon the subject. The beautiful lawns around his country house at Sayes Court, near Deptford, were probably mowed with the diminutive primitive scythe, which cost much time and physical exertion.

When Peter the Great was in England he wantonly devastated these grounds. Evelyn complained of it so bitterly that the Government compensated him for the injury done to his property.

Later we read of the beautiful lawns and artificial lake of Kenilworth Castle.

Great attention is paid to the parks and lawns surrounding the country seats in this country and in Europe.

During the warlike times of ruder ages the castles of the nobility were perched upon almost inaccessible hills, on whose rocky heights scarcely a blade of grass could grow. Now, however, a smoothly-shaven lawn is as necessary an adjunct to the houses of the rich and tasteful as the most and precipitous paths used to be to the castles of the feudal barons.

The tasteful grouping of trees, shrubbery, fountains and statues around our National Capitol, the sloping lawns and well-kept terraces, the ornamental walls that enclose it, are, taken all together, a masterpiece of the art of "landscape gardening."

The great interest taken in reaping and cutting machines, especially between the years 1851 and 1855, in this country, caused the old-fashioned scythe to be superseded by the cylindrical lawn mower.

An apparatus consisting of reciprocating shears was patented in 1800, but was not successful.

The most popular form of the modern lawn mower has a revolving cylinder, armed with spiral knives, which rotate in contact with the rectilinear edge of a stationary knife placed tangentially thereto. The cylinder is rotated by gear connection to the supporting and driving wheels. The machine is made of different sizes to cut a swath of from 18 to 36 inches, and is pushed before him by the gardener.

AGRICULTURAL IMPLEMENTS

1,943 Manufactories in the United States

	1860	1880
Capital Invested . . .	$11,477,239.00	$62,109,668.00
Value of Productions, ...	17,599,960.00	68,640,486.00
Wages Paid, ...	5,080,549.00	15,359,610.00
Hands Employed . . .	14,814	39,480

SUB CLASS

LAWN MOWERS

47,661 Manufactured in 1880

	Primitive Mode	Present Machine
CAPACITY—		
Acres per day, ...	1	7
Hands Employed per day	1	1

138 Patents Granted by the United States

LAWN MOWERS

1. Hand.
2. English—A. D. 1830.
3. U. S. Patent, Reciprocating Knife—A. D. 1861.
4. U. S. Patent, Reciprocating Knife—A. D. 1863.
5. U. S. Patent, Spiral Cutter—A. D. 1868.
6. U. S. Patent, Spiral Cutter—A. D. 1874.
7. U. S. Patent, Edge Trimmer—A. D. 1879.
8. U. S. Patent, Edge Trimmer—A. D. 1883.
9. U. S. Patent, Revolving Cutter—A. D. 1884.

1

2

3

4

5

6

7

8

9

MOWERS

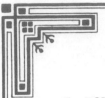

MOWING was a familiar day in Palestine, and the Scripture reference to it shows that "the ardent sun" cured the grass in a short time.

Of the scythe, Pliny says, A. D. 79, "there are two varieties, the Italian, one handed, which is shorter and can be handled among brushwood, and the two-handled Gallic."

The first patent granted by the United States for cutting grain and grass bears date May 17, 1803, to Richard French and J. T. Hawkins, of New Jersey.

A mower which had some popularity was invented by Wm. Manning, of New Jersey, in 1831.

Obed Hussey, of Cincinnati, Ohio, in 1833, patented a machine for reaping and cutting all kinds of grain, to which he applied the saw toothed cutters and guards. This machine was publicly exhibited in 1837.

Cyrus McCormick built one hundred and fifty mowers in 1845.

Whilst the names of Smith, Bell, Gladstone, and Scott are well known in connection with the experimental working of this machine in England, the names of Hussey, McCormick, Ketchum, Manny, Adams, and Ten Eyck are equally familiar to the American farmer as the inventors of mowers and reapers.

The mower and reaper had not attracted much attention until the exhibition of American machines at London, in 1852.

The earliest mowing machines made would cut only dry and coarse grass, and work on uplands, and it was thought until a few years ago that it would be impossible to mow grass while the dew was on. A good machine of the present day, however, will mow in all kinds of grass, whether wet or dry, coarse or fine, and some builders warrant their machines to work well in any place where the farmer is willing to ride.

Though the mowing machine was suggested by the ancient Romans, it is believed that the first experiments tending toward practical results were made in Europe in the early part of the present century, while for its general usefulness and present perfection, the world has acknowledged its obligations to the genius and enterprise of American inventors.

The American mower is awarded the palm of superiority the world over.

72,090 mowers were produced in the United States in 1880.

It is said that there are over 300,000 mowers in use at the present time.

MOWERS

1. Primitive Hand Scythe.
2. English Mower—A. D. 1799.
3. U. S. Patent, Mower—A. D. 1822.
4. U. S. Patent, Slotted Guard Finger and Mower—A. D. 1833.
5. U. S. Patent, Spokeless Wheel Mower—A. D. 1857.
6. U. S. Patent, Front Cut One-Wheel Mower—A. D. 1857.
7. U. S. Patent, Front Cut Two-Wheeled Mower—A. D. 1858.
8. U. S. Patent, Rear Cut One-Wheeled Mower—A. D. 1858.
9. U. S. Patent, Front Center Cut Mower—A. D. 1863.
10. U. S. Patent, Steam Mower—A. D. 1868.
11. U. S. Patent, Front Cut Two-Wheeled Mower—A. D. 1880.
12. U. S. Patent, Front Cut Two-Wheeled Mower—A. D. 1884.

AGRICULTURAL IMPLEMENTS
1,943 Manufactories in the United States

	1860	1880
Capital Invested ...	$11,477,239.00	$62,109,668.00
Value of Productions, ...	17,599,960.00	68,640,486.00
Wages Paid, ...	5,080,549.00	15,359,610.00
Hands Employed ...	14,814	39,480

SUB CLASS
MOWERS
72,090 Manufactured in 1880

	Primitive Mode	Present Machine
CAPACITY—		
Acres per day,....	1 1/2	30
Hands Employed per day, ...	1	1

1,170 Patents Granted by the United States

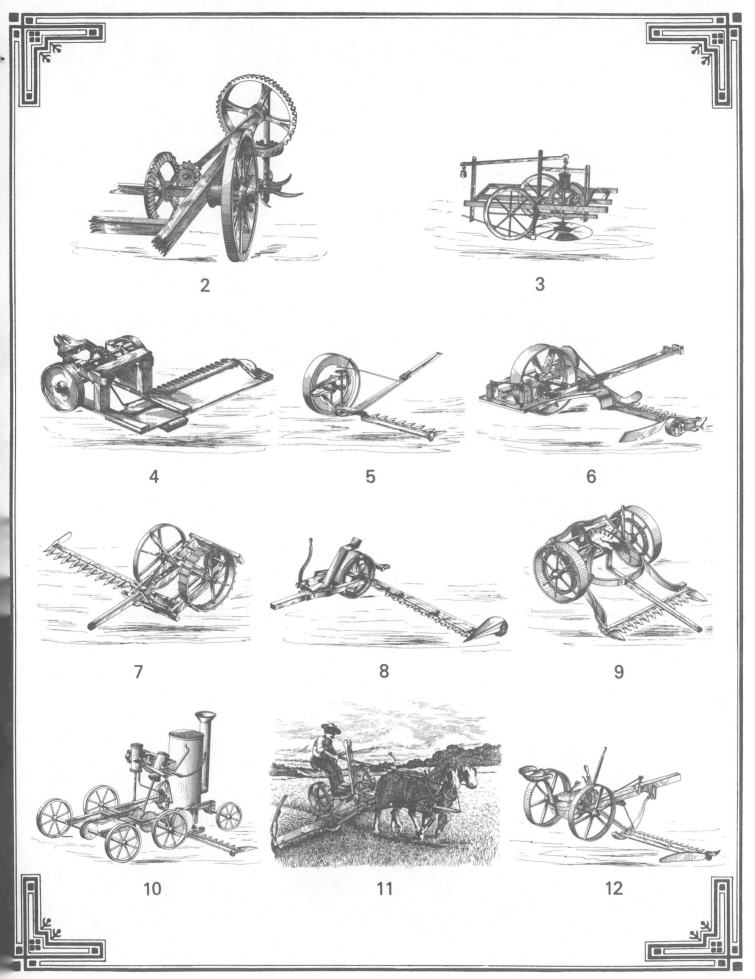

2

3

4

5

6

7

8

9

10

11

12

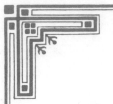

REAPERS

FREQUENT reference is made in the Bible to reaping, and the sickle wherewith the grain was cut.

The Greeks added nothing, and the Romans very little, to the crude mode of cutting grain by the curved sickle of Egypt.

Gleaning was the common privilege of the poor Egyptians and Israelites, and it is ordained by the law of Moses that "When ye reap of the harvest of your land thou shalt not make clean riddance of the corners of the field; neither shalt thou gather any gleanings of the harvest; thou shalt leave them to the poor and to the stranger."

The Gauls used the reaper A. D. 70. Pliny says that "in the extensive fields in the lowlands of Gaul, vans (carts) of large size, with projecting teeth on the edge, are driven on two wheels through the standing grain by an ox, yoked in a reverse position; in this manner the ears are torn off and fall into the van."

Palladius also wrote a description of this machine in the 4th century.

After a lapse of centuries this form of machine is used for gathering clover.

The first modern machine was similar to the Gallic.

The English machine of Pitt, 1786, had a cylinder, on which were rows of combs which tore off the ears and discharged them in a box of the machine.

In 1799 Boyce, of England, invented the vertical shaft with rotary scythe.

Mr. Gladstone, in 1806, was the first to use the horse in front, beside the uncut grain.

The invention of Henry Ogle, in 1822, marks the commencement of a new era in reaping machines, his machine was of extreme simplicity and used a reciprocating cutter.

The Bell machine, of 1826, which was brought forward to confound the American exhibitors at the World's Fair, held at London, 1857, was pushed ahead of the horses.

In this machine there was the adjustable reel—a method of raising the cutters, and also a mode of delivering the cut grass in line on the ground, to allow any number of binders to work after it.

In the summer of 1855 a competitive trial of reapers took place in France; the competitors were America and England. The American machine cut an acre in 22 minutes; the English machine cut an acre in 66 minutes.

There were produced in the United States in the year 1880 35,327 reaping machines.

AGRICULTURAL IMPLEMENTS

1,943 Manufactories in the United States

	1860	1880
Capital Invested . . .	$11,477,239.00	$62,109,668.00
Value of Productions, ...	17,599,960.00	68,640,486.00
Wages Paid, ...	5,080,549.00	15,359,610.00
Hands Employed . . .	14,814	39,480

SUB CLASS
REAPERS

35,327 Manufactured in 1880

	Primitive Mode	Present Machine
CAPACITY—		
Acres per day, ...	1 1/2	20
Hands Employed per day, ...	1	1

1,398 Patents Granted by the United States

REAPERS

1. Egyptian Sickle.
2. Colonial Sickle.
3. Grain Cradle.
4. English—A. D. 1799.
5. U. S. Patent, Harvester—A.D. 1834.
6. U. S. Patent, Harvester, Hand Raker—A. D. 1855.
7. U. S. Patent, Harvester, Self Raker—A. D. 1856.
8. U. S. Patent, Harvester, Dropper—A. D. 1861.
9. U. S. Patent, Adjustable Switch Reel Rake—A. D. 1865.
10. U. S. Patent, Adjustable Switch Reel Rake—A. D. 1875.
11. U. S. Patent, Adjustable Switch Reel Rake—A. D. 1879.
12. U. S. Patent, Adjustable Switch Reel Rake—A. D. 1884.

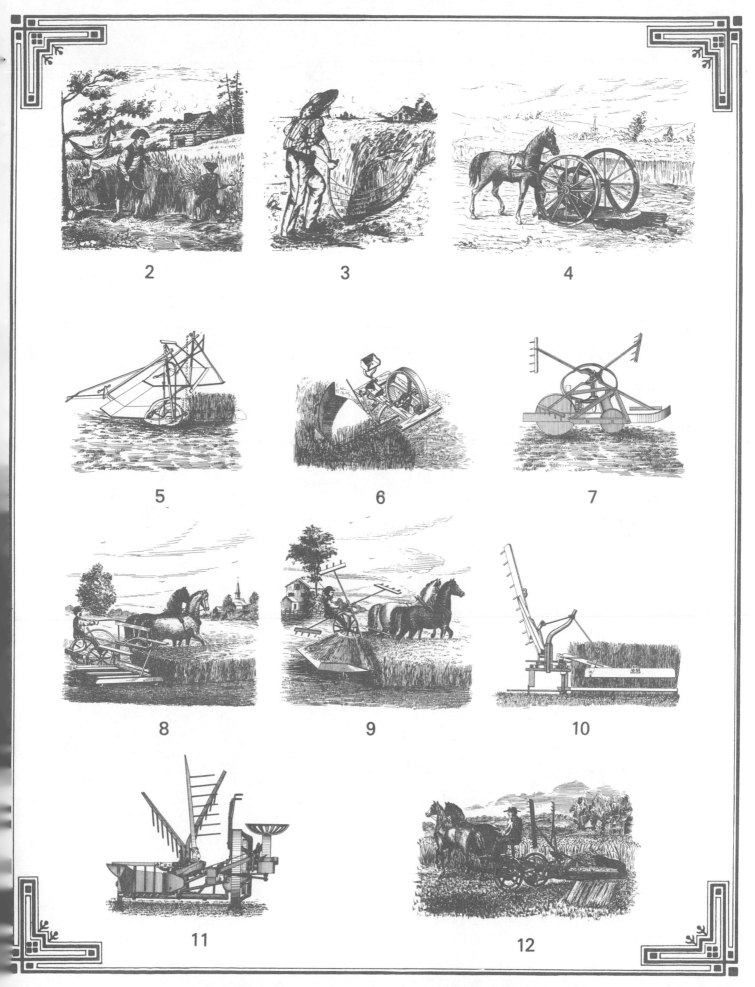

2

3

4

5

6

7

8

9

10

11

12

COMBINED REAPERS AND THRASHERS

UNDER another head is given a full history of harvester cutting apparatus, carrying the reader back to the most ancient devices for cutting grain. An appliance which at once reaps and thrashes is of comparatively modern invention.

In 1828 Samuel Lane, of Maine, invented a reaper with which a thrasher was combined. This combination arrangement has not, however, yet come into general use.

In the State of California the combined reaper and thrasher is found to be more available, as the special conditions of the topography, soil and climate make its use practicable.

The steam harvester is used in all the grain fields of the great West. This cuts the grain in broad swaths, and with incredible rapidity; it is thrashed by the same power.

A portable engine, by whose power the reaper is first propelled and afterwards the thrasher, has been found to be the most convenient method of harvesting the larger crops of grain. The reaper of Cyrus W. McCormick, after which the most notable modern machines may be said to have been modeled, combined, perhaps, more desirable qualities than any others. In this machine, although the reaping and thrashing are not done simultaneously, the grain is so compactly bound as it is reaped that the thrashing can be speedily and conveniently accomplished.

AGRICULTURAL IMPLEMENTS
1,943 Manufactories in the United States

	1860	1880
Capital Invested . . .	$11,477,239.00	$62,109,668.00
Value of Productions, ...	17,599,960.00	68,640,486.00
Wages Paid, ...	5,080,549.00	15,359,610.00
Hands Employed . . .	14,814	39,480

SUB CLASS
COMBINED REAPERS AND THRASHERS
44 Patents Granted by the United States

COMBINED REAPERS AND THRASHERS

1. U. S. Patent, Reaper and Thrasher—A. D. 1836.
2. U. S. Patent, Thrasher, Separator and Sacker—A. D. 1846.
3. U. S. Patent, Head Cutter and Side Deliver—A. D. 1849.
4. U. S. Patent, Harvester and Thrasher—A. D. 1877.
5. U. S. Patent, Steam Harvester—A. D. 1879.
6. U. S. Patent, Header, Thrasher and Separator—A. D. 1883.

1

2

3

4

5

6

HARVESTER BINDERS

THE most primitive method of binding grain was a wisp or bunch of the grain twisted and tied around the bundle. These bundles were stacked together in what are called "sheaves."

A great many experiments have been made to produce a machine which will bind grain as fast as it is cut.

Among the first to succeed at this was Allen Sherwood, of Auburn, N. Y., who was granted a patent for a grain binder in 1858.

A simple sheaf binder is a string strained around a sheaf by means of a notched stick. The band is composed of the two cords knotted together, forming loops.

At the Paris exposition a number of cord and wire binders were exhibited. One exhibitor showed a cord made of twisted bark of osiers; another showed cheap hempen cords in packages of 1,000 each. It was demonstrated that there was a waste in using a bunch of the grain as a binder.

Another patented device is a grain band having a string attached to a block. Both are treated with tar, and are smoked to render them undestructible by humidity, and noxious to insects.

At the Paris exposition in 1878 there were exhibited nine binding reapers—six American and three British. Four American machines went into the field, all of which used the wire binder. Since then each of the owners has placed a twine binder on the market instead. Two twine binders were shown at this exposition, one American and one British, but did not compete on the field. The four competing machines were those of McCormick, Wood, Osborne and Aultman. In the McCormick twine-binding reaper the cut grain is delivered upon a platform, which is a moving web of canvas, which carries it to the elevated aprons and then delivers it upon the binding table. Here a band is placed around the middle of the bundle, tied closely, and the twine or wire cut.

The binding apparatus consists of a needle arm, gripper and discharging device, with the necessary gear. The needle rises through the table when the grain is in place, carrying the twine with it; this encircles the sheaf and a quick knot is tied. The twine string is fed from a tin canister on top of the machine, which can be worked by one man.

The reaping and automatic machine of S. D. Locke, of New York, made by Walter Wood, of that State, is believed to be the most perfect binder, after twelve years of experiment. Since 1874 great numbers of these machines have been put upon the market and are now in successful operation.

Among other successful binders is that of James F. Gordon, of New York, patented in 1874.

Barta's self-binder has also worked successfully. It uses cord and makes a square knot. This is also a recent invention.

HARVESTER BINDERS

1. U. S. Patent, Cord Knotter—A. D. 1853.
2. U. S. Patent, Wire Twister—A. D. 1856.
3. U. S. Patent, Straw Braid Twister—A. D. 1857.
4. U. S. Patent, Gleaner and Binder—A. D. 1862.
5. U. S. Patent, Self Tripping Cord Knotter—A. D. 1867.
6. U. S. Patent, Wire Twister—A. D. 1868.
7. U. S. Patent, Automatic Trip—A. D. 1870.
8. U. S. Patent, Straw Looper—A. D. 1870.
9. U. S. Patent, Vibrating Binder—A. D. 1875.
10. U. S. Patent, Low Down Binder—A. D. 1878.
11. U. S. Patent, Compressor Automatic Trip—A. D. 1879.
12. U. S. Patent, Low Down Oblique Delivery—A. D. 1884.

AGRICULTURAL IMPLEMENTS

1,943 Manufactories in the United States

	1860	1880
Capital Invested ...	$11,477,239.00	$62,109,668.00
Value of Productions, ...	17,599,960.00	68,640,486.00
Wages Paid,.......	5,080,549.00	15,359,610.00
Hands Employed ...	14,814	39,480

SUB CLASS
HARVESTER BINDERS

	Primitive Mode	Present Machine
Acres per day,....	1/2	20
Hands Employed per day, ...	1	1

697 Patents Granted by the United States

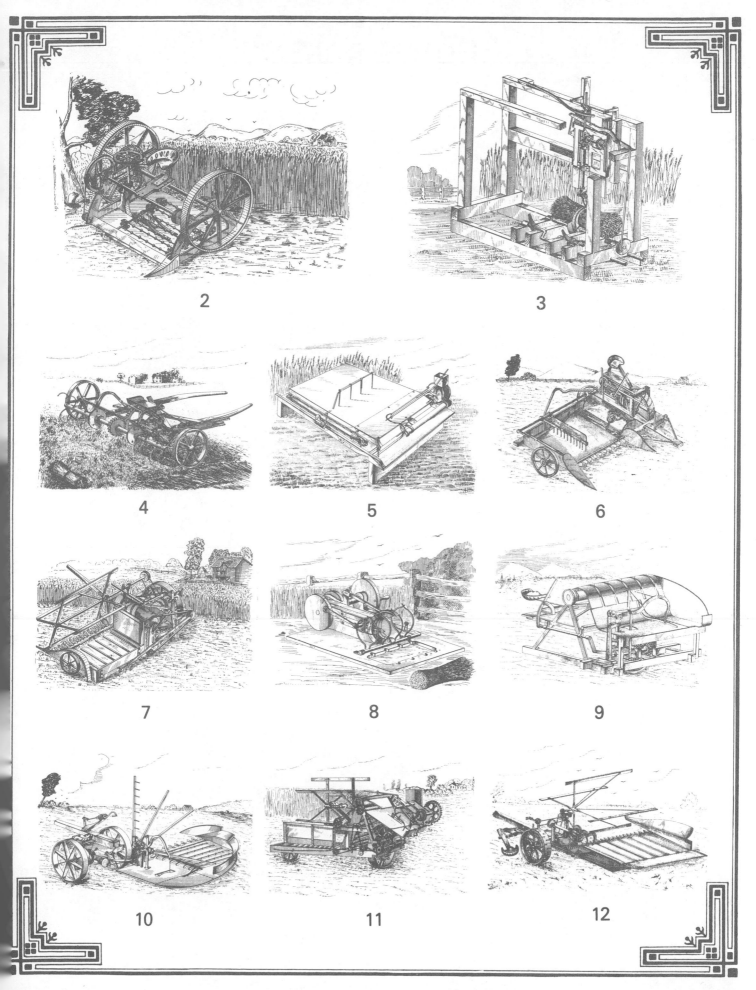

2

3

4

5

6

7

8

9

10

11

12

THE rake is not represented in the sculptures of ancient Egypt.

Grain rakes in Great Britain are made of large size, for raking and gleaning the stubble. The head is four feet long, the teeth of iron four inches long and one and one-half inches apart.

In Scotland a rake is used with a jointed head fifteen feet long; the handle has a cross-bar, and the implement is drawn by two men.

The wheeled hand rake of the United States used for grain or hay was the precursor of the modern horse rake.

The American horse rake with curved steel tires attached to a bar hinged to a light axle tree, was first used in Pennsylvania.

Those having two sets of wooden teeth lying close to the earth and revolving at the will of the driver, were invented by H. N. Tracy, of Vermont.

Horse rakes are of several kinds, and have come into extensive use of late years. They are wheeled or wheelers.

Some rake heads revolve as in the flop-over rake, in others the rake head is formed by, or attached to, the axle or trails behind it, and the teeth are only lifted to deliver the hay.

In some the teeth are independent, so as to yield to obstacles without affecting the operation of the other teeth. The rake head in some cases is turned by hand at the proper moment, but is more commonly arranged to receive motion from the power of the animal when a holding device is released by the driver.

The mower, horse rake, and hay fork are a most effective trio in the business of cutting and saving hay.

AGRICULTURAL IMPLEMENTS

1,943 Manufactories in the United States

	1860	1880
Capital Invested ...	$11,477,239.00	$62,109,668.00
Value of Productions, ...	17,599,960.00	68,640,486.00
Wages Paid, ...	5,080,549.00	15,359,610.00
Hands Employed ...	14,814	39,480

SUB CLASS
HORSE RAKES

95,625 Manufactured in 1880

	Primitive Mode	Present Machine
CAPACITY—		
Acres per day, ...	5	30
Hands Employed per day........	1	1

963 Patents Granted by the United States

HORSE RAKES

1. Primitive, Hand.
2. U. S. Patent, Flopover—A. D. 1822.
3. U. S. Patent, Spring Tooth—A. D. 1839.
4. U. S. Patent, Dumping Sulky—A. D. 1848.
5. U. S. Patent, Draft Dumping—A. D. 1850.
6. U. S. Patent, Self Dumping—A. D. 1852.
7. U. S. Patent, Spring Tooth Self Dumping—A. D. 1856.
8. U. S. Patent, Draft Dumping—A. D. 1856.
9. U. S. Patent, Draft Dumping—A. D. 1859.
10. U. S. Patent, Drag Dumping—A. D. 1866.
11. U. S. Patent, Draft Dumping—A. D. 1866.
12. U. S. Patent, Drag Dumping—A. D. 1870.
13. U. S. Patent, Draft Dumping—A. D. 1876.
14. U. S. Patent, Draft Dumping—A. D. 1884.

1

2

3

4

5

6

7

8

9

10

11

12

HAY FORKS

THE fork of the husbandman is shown on Egyptian tombs, and is referred to in the Book of Judges, 1093 B. C.: "Yet they had a file for the mattocks and for the colters and for the forks."

They are classified in the U. S. Patent Office as hay forks, proper; hay forks, corkscrew; hay forks, grapple; hay forks, harpoon; hay forks, tilting.

HAY FORKS

476 Patents Granted by the United States

HAY FORKS

1. Primitive, Hand.
2. U. S. Patent, Spiral Horse Fork—A. D. 1867.
3. U. S. Patent, Harpoon Horse Fork—A. D. 1867.
4. U. S. Patent, Tilting Horse Fork—A. D. 1870.
5. U. S. Patent, Grapple Horse Fork—A. D. 1880.
6. U. S. Patent, Harpoon Horse Fork—A. D. 1881.
7. U. S. Patent, Hand Fork—A. D. 1882.
8. U. S. Patent, Harpoon Horse Fork—A. D. 1884.
9. U. S. Patent, Harpoon Horse Fork—A. D. 1884.

2

1

3

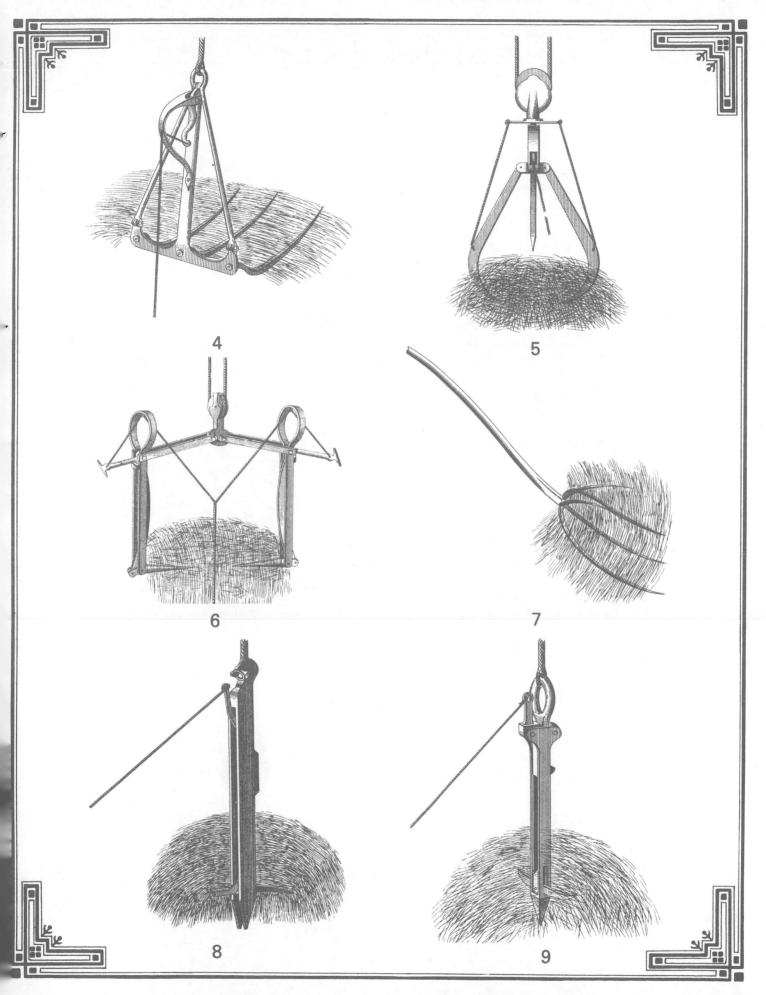

4

5

6

7

8

9

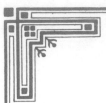

HAY LOADERS

HAY is commonly made of grasses, a few leguminous plants, and clover.

Plants are in the best state to be cut for fodder when in blossom, or just out of blossom.

The cutting of grass for hay is done by hand scythes, or horse power and steam-propelled machines.

The swaths are shaken out and exposed to the sun by machines called tedders or spreaders. When dry the hay is raked together by horse rakes into long heaps called "windrows." These "windrows" are divided and formed into conical heaps and called "cocks."

Horse hay forks were originally used to hoist the hay on the wagons and into barns. These hay forks are arranged so that by a system of ropes, blocks and rods, the hay is lifted from the load upon the forks and delivered in any section of the barn.

The inventive genius of this century has perfected a machine after many trials, by which the "windrows" are speedily gathered up and lifted through a series of spiral attachments to a point above the hay wagon, whence it is deposited in the wagon.

This invention can be worked either by steam or horse power. The work is done with great rapidity and thoroughness. In isolated districts the old-fashioned hay fork is still used, but improvements in the shape and capacity of the fork are apparent.

HAY LOADERS

1. Primitive, Hand.
2. U. S. Patent, Raker and Loader—A. D. 1848.
3. U. S. Patent, Raker and Loader—A. D. 1850.
4. U. S. Patent, Reel Raker and Loader—A. D. 1858.
5. U. S. Patent, Walking Reel Loader—A. D. 1860.
6. U. S. Patent, Endless Belt Loader—A. D. 1861.
7. U. S. Patent, Side Delivering Raker and Loader—A. D. 1864.
8. U. S. Patent, Lifting Drag Rake Loader—A. D. 1865.
9. U. S. Patent, Raker and Loader—A. D. 1867.
10. U. S. Patent, Intermittent Action Loader—A. D. 1868.
11. U. S. Patent, Spiral Elevator—A. D. 1870.
12. U. S. Patent, Raker and Loader—A. D. 1876.
13. U. S. Patent, Raker and Loader—A. D. 1883.

1

AGRICULTURAL IMPLEMENTS

1,943 Manufactories in the United States

	1860	1880
Capital Invested ...	$11,477,239.00	$62,109,668.00
Value of Productions, ...	17,599,960.00	68,640,486.00
Wages Paid, ...	5,080,549.00	15,359,610.00
Hands Employed ...	14,814	39,480

SUB CLASS
HAY LOADERS

8,957 Manufactured in 1880

	Primitive Mode	Present Machine
CAPACITY—		
Tons per day, ...	4	25
Hands Employed per day, ...	2	2

266 Patents Granted by the United States

2

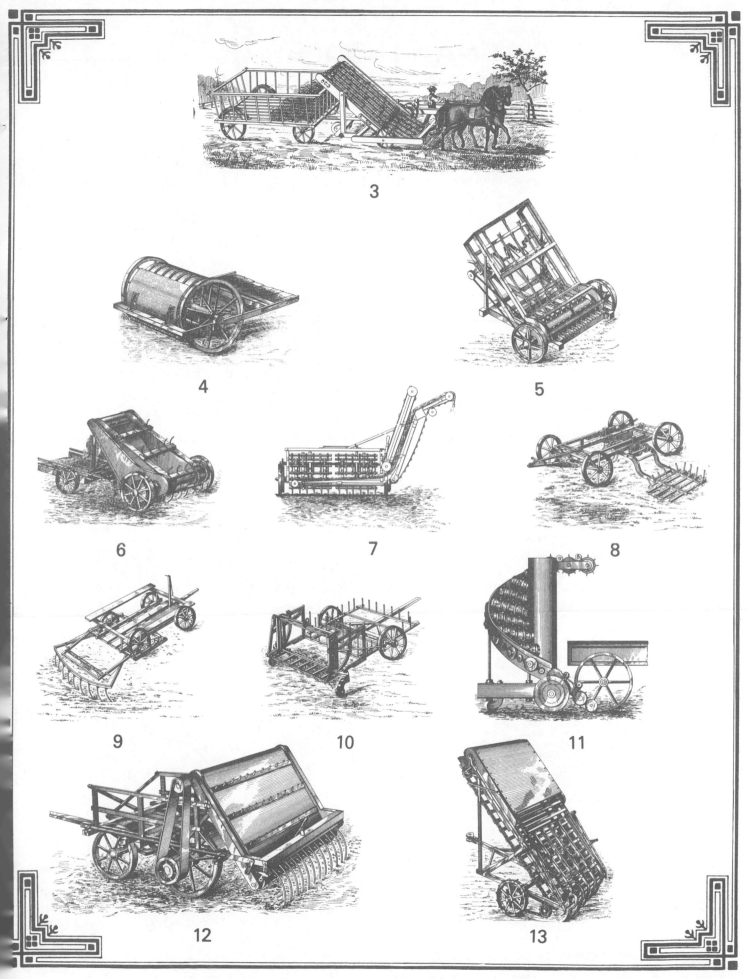

3

4

5

6

7

8

9

10

11

12

13

HAY TEDDERS

THE hay tedder was invented about 1800 by Salmon, of England, and is more useful in the humid climate of that country than the United States. It consists of a pair of wheels supporting a reel, consisting of an open cylindrical frame, formed by arms proceeding from it and carrying bars set with curved tines pointing outward. This reel may be lifted out of operative position when going to and from work in the field, and when at work it is rotated by a pinion connection to a spur wheel in the hub of one wheel.

By the use of the modern tedder, which upturns the new-cut and half-cured grass as it lies upon the ground and promotes its more rapid curing, the risk of exposures to summer storms is greatly lessened.

1

AGRICULTURAL IMPLEMENTS
1,943 Manufactories in the United States

	1860	1880
Capital Invested . . .	$11,477,239.00	$62,109,668.00
Value of Productions, ...	17,599,960.00	68,640,486.00
Wages Paid, ...	5,080,549.00	15,359,610.00
Hands Employed . . .	14,814	39,480

SUB CLASS
HAY TEDDERS
2,334 Manufactured in 1880.

	Primitive Mode	Present Machine
CAPACITY— Acres per day, ...	5	40
Hands Employed per day, ...	1	1

122 Patents Granted by the United States

HAY TEDDERS

1. Hand.
2. U. S. Patent, Tedder—A. D. 1855.
3. U. S. Patent, Tedder—A. D. 1861.
4. U. S. Patent, Tedder—A. D. 1862.
5. U. S. Patent, Rake and Tedder—A. D. 1865.
6. U. S. Patent, Rake and Tedder—A. D. 1867.
7. U. S. Patent, Rake and Tedder—A.D. 1870.
8. U. S. Patent, Tedder—A. D. 1883.

2

3

4

5

6

7

8

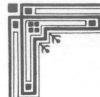

THRASHING AND CLEANING GRAIN

OXEN were anciently employed in thrashing corn, and the same custom is still retained in Egypt and the east. This operation is effected by trampling upon the sheaves, and by dragging a clumsy machine, furnished with three rollers. A wooden chair is attached to the machine, and on this a driver seats himself, urging his oxen backwards and forwards among the sheaves, which have previously been thrown into a heap of about eight feet wide and two in height. The grain thus beaten out is collected in an open place, and shaken against the wind by an attendant with a small shovel, or, as it is termed, a winnowing fan, which disperses the chaff and leaves the grain uninjured.

Horace further tells us that the thrashing floor was mostly a smooth space, surrounded with mud walls, having a barn or garner on one side; occasionally an open field, outside the walls, was selected for this purpose, yet uniformly before the town or city gates. Such was the void place wherein the "King of Israel, and Jehoshaphat, King of Judah sat, each of them on his throne, clothed in his robes, at the entering in of the gate of Samaria, and all the prophets prophesied before them."

In the marginal reading we are informed that this void space was no other than a thrashing floor; and truly the area was well adapted for such an assemblage, being equally suited to accommodate the two kings and their attendants, and to separate them for the populace.

A four-horse power portable engine with six-inch cylinder, pressure of steam 45 pounds per square inch, revolutions, 140 per minute, has thrashed, under favorable surroundings, 320 bushels per day of ten hours; coal consumed 3 cwt. Another engine, of five horse power, thrashed 400 bushels; coal consumed 4 cwt. Another, of six-horse power, thrashed 480 bushels; coal consumed 5 cwt. Another, of seven-horse power, thrashed 560 bushels; coal consumed 6 cwt. Another, of eight-horse power, thrashed 640 bushels; coal consumed 7 cwt. Another of ten-horse power, thrashed 800 bushels per day; coal consumed 9 cwt.

The economy of these performances is evident at a glance, and even if much less work than the above was effected, such an engine would, if mounted on wheels, prove a most valuable acquisition to any neighborhood composed of thrifty farmers, who might, by an equitable arrangement, become both the owners and beneficiaries of the same.

THRASHING AND CLEANING GRAIN

1. Egyptian—1500 B. C.
2. Roman Tribulum—100 B. C.
3. Hand Flail.
4. Horse Thrashing.
5. Flail Thrashing Machine.
6. U. S. Patent, Horse Power, A. D. 1834.
7. U. S. Patent, Steam Power, A. D. 1883.

AGRICULTURAL IMPLEMENTS
1,943 Manufactories in the United States

	1860	1880
Capital Invested ...	$11,477,239.00	$62,109,668.00
Value of Productions, ...	17,599,960.00	68,640,486.00
Wages Paid, ...	5,080,549.00	15,359,610.00
Hands Employed ...	14,814	39,480

SUB CLASS
THRASHING AND CLEANING GRAIN
19,527 Machines Manufactured in 1880

	Primitive Mode	Present Machine
CAPACITY—		
Bushels Wheat per day, ...	20	1,000
Bushels Oats per day, ...	40	2,000
Hands Employed per day, ...	4	4

Grain Threshed, 1883, 1,540,000 Bushels

2,615 Patents Granted by the United States

2

3

4

5

6

7

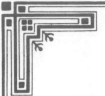

WINNOWING AND SIFTING GRAIN

THE winnowing of grain is early mentioned in Sacred History. "The oxen likewise and the young asses that ear the ground shall eat clean provender, which hath been removed with the shovel and with the fan. (Isaiah xxx,24.) "Like as grain is sifted with a sieve." (Amos ix, 9.)

The oldest representations that we have of the process of winnowing is on the Egyptian tombs, where men with scoops are throwing the grain up in the air so that the passing wind may drive off the chaff.

The Egyptians used sifters made of papyrus, the ancient Spaniards of flax, and the Gauls invented sieves of horse hair.

In Britain the use of the hand sieve riddle was the only method employed for dressing grain until the last century.

We derive the winnowing machine from Britain, which country obtained it from Holland. In 1710 it was introduced into Scotland by Meikle, the father of Meikle who invented the thrashing machine.

The English word is derived from the idea of making an artificial blast by means of a fan, and the specific mechanical purpose is to separate grain from chaff by a blast of wind acting upon the latter, which is lighter than the grain.

It is among the histories of the machine that when it was introduced into Scotland certain sensitive persons pronounced it an impious device, as "It raised a wind when the Lord had made a calm." This is but another form of the opposition which met Kepler and Galileo.

Gooch, of England, in 1800, invented the more modern machine which embraces the important features of the rotating fan, the shaking riddle and sieves, for assorting grain and separating extraneous substances. Winnowing machines are frequently attached to thrashing machines.

Winnowing machines, oftener called "fanning mills" in this country, are machines in which grain, accompanied by chaff, dirt, cockle, grass, seeds, dust and straw, is subjected to a shaking action, or riddled and sieved in succession. An artificial blast of wind is driven against it on and through the seives as it falls.

WINNOWING AND SIFTING GRAIN

1. Primitive Winnowing, Egypt—1500 B. C.
2. Primitive Winnowing, Rome—100 B. C.
3. English Fanning Mill—A. D. 1775.
4. U. S. Patent, Fanning Mill—A. D. 1829.
5. U. S. Patent, Fanning Mill—A. D. 1879.
6. U. S. Patent, Air Separator—A.D. 1881.
7. U. S. Patent, Rolling Screen—A. D. 1884.
8. U. S. Patent, Cockle Machine—A. D. 1884.

1

2

WINNOWING AND SIFTING GRAIN

1,038 Patents Granted by the United States

3

4

5

6

7

8

CORN HUSKERS, SHELLERS, AND HOMINY MAKING

THE North American Indians pounded their maize in mortars, to make a coarse meal or hominy.

Some corn husking machines operate upon the corn in the field to husk it off the stalk; and the machine tears off the husks from the ears.

In the hominy mill or machine the corn is subjected to a grating or beating action, which removes the cuticle and the germ, and by persistent and sufficiently energetic action, may break the grain as small as may be wanted. The sizes are graded by sifting.

It is said that the old hand process of shelling corn would require the entire population of the United States 6 days in the week—100 days per year—to shell the corn crop.

The cultivating and milling of rice in Louisiana gives employment to a large percentage of the population. There are about 900 rice plantations in the State. New Orleans has twelve mills, with a capacity for cleaning 275,000 barrels per annum.

CORN HUSKERS, SHELLERS, AND HOMINY MAKING

1. Primitive Corn Husker.
2. Primitive Hominy Mortar.
3. Primitive Corn Sheller.
4. English Hominy Mill—A. D. 1715.
5. U. S. Patent, Corn Sheller—A. D. 1815.
6. U. S. Patent, Corn Husker—A. D. 1837.
7. U. S. Patent, Hominy Machine—A. D. 1868.
8. U. S. Patent, Corn Sheller—A. D. 1882.
9. U. S. Patent, Husker—A. D. 1883.

AGRICULTURAL IMPLEMENTS

1,943 Manufactories in the United States

	1860	1880
Capital Invested . . .	$11,477,239.00	$62,109,668.00
Value of Productions, ...	17,599,960.00	68,640,486.00
Wages Paid, ...	5,080,549.00	15,359,610.00
Hands Employed . . .	14,814	39,480

SUB CLASS
CORN HUSKERS, SHELLERS, AND HOMINY MAKING

	Primitive Mode	Present Machine
CAPACITY—		
Bushels per day, . .	10	1,000
Hands Employed per day, ...	1	1

682 Patents Granted by the United States

1

2

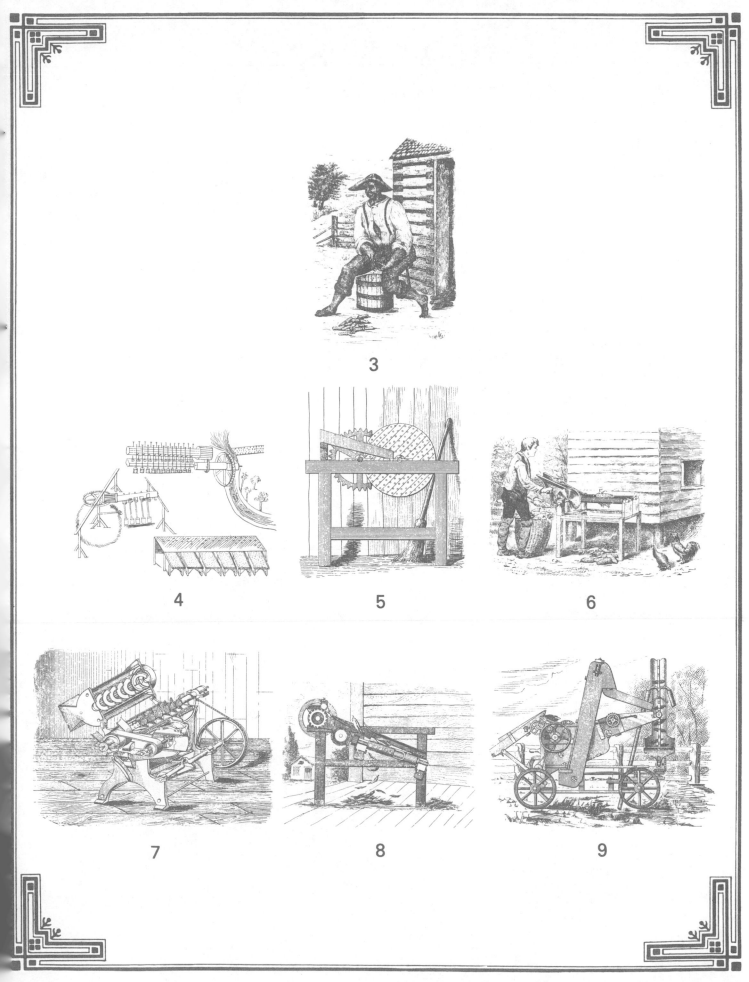

3

4   5   6

7   8   9

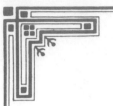
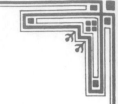

WHEAT, RICE AND COTTON SEED HULLERS

THE decortication of grain was practiced by the Romans, the whole grain being pounded in mortars with some abradant, which rasped off the cuticle.

In the time of Pliny, a mortar was employed for hulling grain, sand or pieces of brick being placed therein to assist the trituration, foreign substances, such as the husk and bran, being removed by sifting.

Mills for the manufacture of pearl barley were invented in Germany, and first used in Holland in 1660.

The Scotch pearl barley mill consists of a drum, which is rotated by suitable gearing, and within which a circular grindstone is caused to rapidly revolve. The grain is fed through a hopper, opening axially into the drum, and is removed by a sluice at its side. The drum is lined with sheet iron, perforated with small holes, which serve to remove the skin and a portion of the outer substance of the grain, bringing it to a spheroidal shape.

Other varieties of machines depend partly upon percussion.

Mills for decorticating are known in England as barley mills.

Rough rice has an outer husk and a thin cuticle which adheres to the pearly grain with great tenacity. The old mode of hulling rice was by pounding in mortars, which were made of wood, holding from one to two bushels.

Lucas, in 1780, constructed a machine driven by tide power, which operated iron shod pestles in cast iron mortars, holding five bushels each of rough rice.

Ewbanks rice huller was one of the first introduced, and was patented in England in 1819.

Steam machines succeeded the hand machines, and are now mostly used for hulling rice.

The cotton seed huller is a modern device, by which the hull of the cotton seed is rasped off and sifted from the farinaceous and oily matters, which are utilized for their oil, and the refuse is used for fertilizers.

WHEAT, RICE AND COTTON SEED HULLERS

613 Patents Granted by the United States

WHEAT, RICE AND COTTON SEED HULLERS

1. Primitive Rice Mortar.
2. Chinese Rice Mortar.
3. U. S. Patent, Wheat Huller and Smutter—A. D. 1832.
4. U. S. Patent, Cotton Seed Huller—A. D. 1834.
5. U. S. Patent, Rice Mortar—A. D. 1878.
6. U. S. Patent, Wheat Huller and Smutter—A. D. 1883.
7. U. S. Patent, Cotton Seed Huller—A. D. 1884.
8. U. S. Patent, Rice and Grain Scourer—A. D. 1884.

1

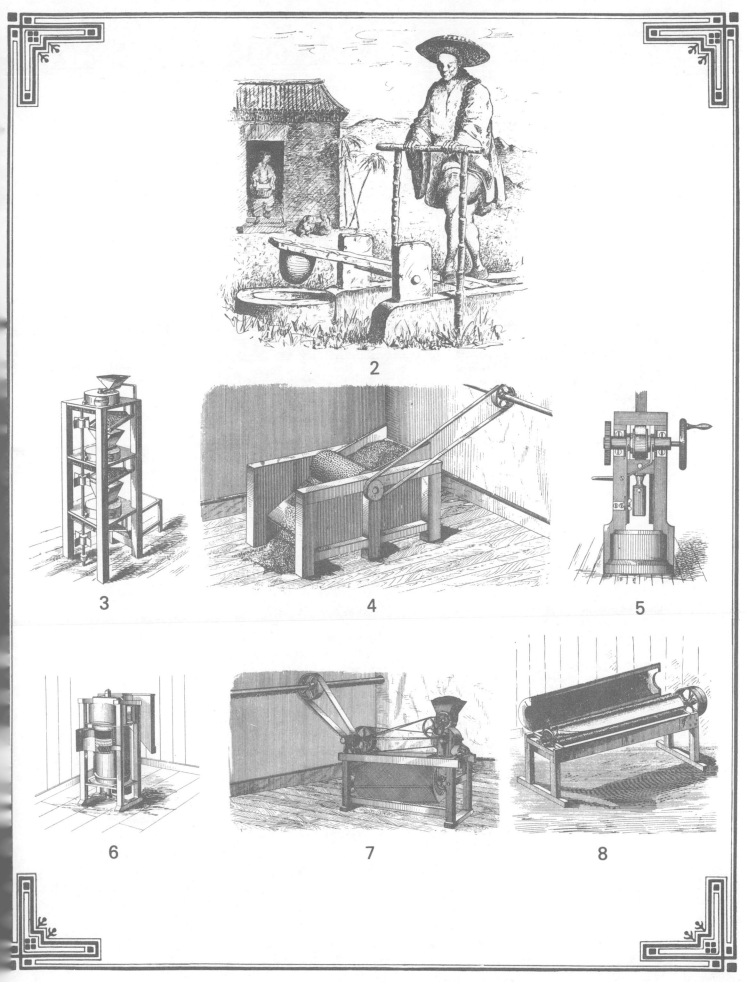

2

3

4

5

6

7

8

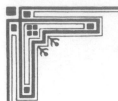

GRAIN CONVEYORS

THE first elevator, disconnected from milling, for transferring and storage of grain, was built by Joseph Dart, of Buffalo, N.Y., U.S., in 1843.

There are many forms of grain conveyors, which generally agree in that they afford means of exposing a shower of grain to a current of highly dried and heated air. The following kinds may be cited, and it must be understood that there are many varieties and modifications of each.

In the conveyor system the grain from the spout passes consecutively through the cylinders, in each of which is a rotating screw conveyor driven by cog-wheels, having for axles hollow perforated tubes, through which the damp air passes from the grain, being drawn by the exhaust fan. The cylinders connect by the spout, and the lower one discharges by the spout. The heated air from the furnace rises into the chamber above and surrounds the cylinders.

In the revolving cup system, the grain enters upon a heated cone, and thence passes to a revolving flanged disk, which distributes it, to be again collected by the hopper, and fed to other disks, and so on, in descending series, to the discharge spout. A current of heated air ascends through the chamber and envelopes the grain at all times.

In the zigzag incline system, the grain descends from a hopper, and is shifted over from side to side by the alternate inclines, which are perforated plates in a flue occupied by an upward current of heated air.

The annular drum system consists of a vertical, double cylindrical chamber with conical ends. The space between the inner and outer casing is the one traversed by the grain, which enters at the apex of the upper and departs at the apex of the lower cone. The inner and outer casings are all perforated with holes, about 2,300 to the square foot, the punching being from without, inward; the slight roughness has a tendency to turn the grain which rubs against the protuberances, giving a sort

of stirring action thereto, and aiding the exposure of its whole surface to the stream of heated-air. The heat is generated by a stove in the interior of the chamber, and the heated air passes through both casings and the body of grain contained between them. The apparatus stands on legs, so as to elevate the discharge opening, that the falling grain may be received into sacks for shipping.

The spiral flue system consists of a long spiral tube traversed by a flue from a stove. The sides of the tube are full of fine perforations, and the draft is upward between the two surfaces, and outward through the perforations, carrying the moisture from the grain, which descends in a shower between the flue pipe and the perforated casing.

The traveling belt system consists of a furnace, air box, and traveling belt, which receives its grain from a hopper. Grain from the hopper falls on a belt which travels over the grated top of the box, which is heated by air from a fan and tubes which form the box and basket grate of the furnace. After passing the length of the box the grain is caught between the belts and returned to the hopper for a repetition of the operation, or as it descends is intercepted by a spout.

In the rotatory drum system an inclined cylinder of wire contains the grain, which tumbles over and over, and is eventually discharged at the lower end of the cylinder, which rotates in a heated chamber.

The largest grain elevator in the United States, and probably in the world, is situated in Brooklyn, New York. It has a storage capacity of 2,500,000, bushels, besides superior transfer facilities and dockage for half a dozen vessels, which can be loaded at one time. The machinery in the elevator can take grain at the rate of 8,000 bushels an hour from the barges or vessels at the pier. The grain is elevated, sifted and fanned, weighed, stored, put in bins, and then transferred to vessels at the pier. There are about five miles of belting, called conveyers. These conveyers travel at the rate of about 600 feet a minute, and carry to its destination 2⅓ bushels of grain a minute.

GRAIN CONVEYORS

	Primitive Mode	Present Machine
CAPACITY—		
Bushels per day, . .	1,000	80,000
Hands Employed		
per day, ... 10	10	

184 Patents Granted by the United States

GRAIN CONVEYORS

1. U. S. Patent, Elevator—A. D. 1834.
2. U. S. Patent, Screw—A. D. 1869.
3. U. S. Patent, Elevator—A. D. 1882.
4. U. S. Patent, Portable—A. D. 1882.
5. U. S. Patent, Pneumatic—A. D. 1883.
6. U. S. Patent, Transfer—A. D. 1883.

1

2

3

4

5

6

CARE OF STOCK

THE care of stock is almost as old as the human race.

In the sculpture of Nimrod is represented a tent within which is a groom currying a horse.

The Arabians are noted for the care they take of their horses, and the result of years of kindness and attention has produced a breed whose beauty, strength, swiftness and enfurance have made it both famous and valuable.

The Hebrews cut straw and grain in the sheaf for food.

Hohlfield, of Saxony, about 1711, invented a straw chopper.

The chaff cutter of the last century was a trough, in which the hay or straw was pushed along by a fork so as to be exposed to a knife at the end of the trough, and was oscillated by hand.

Horses and oxen are fed in a trough arranged in their stalls. The best stock breeders allow each animal a separate trough for food. Their food is now prepared for them by being cut up in different kinds of machines. Fodder is cut very fine. Corn is taken off the ear and the grains are cut in two. Meal for milch cows is soaked in hot water.

Sheep are kept in warmer quarters than formerly, and fed in a way which has greatly increased the quality and quantity of their wool.

A sheep rack has been invented which is of portable wrought iron and is mounted on four wheels. It has a wrought-iron hay rack in the middle, a trough at each side, doors at the ends and a corrugated iron roof with eave gutters.

CARE OF STOCK

Livestock on Farms in the United States

	1860	1880
Horses, ...	6,249,174	10,357,488
Mules and Asses, . .	1,151,148	1,812,808
Working Oxen, ...	2,254,911	933,841
Milch Cows, ...	8,585,735	12,443,120
Other Cattle, ...	14,779,373	22,488,550
Sheep, ...	22,471,275	35,192,074
Swine, ...	33,512,867	47,681,700

Livestock on Ranches and Ranges

Cattle, ...	Not reported.	3,750.022
Sheep, ...	Not reported.	7,000,000
Swine, ...	Not reported.	2,090,970
Value, ...	$1,089,329,915.00	$1,500,384,707.00

1,430 Patents Granted by the United States

A sheep shearing machine has also been invented, which greatly facilitates that unpleasant operation.

A device known as a stock feeder automatically supplies feed to stock in limited quantities at certain times. It is an ingenious, but not commonly adopted, device, attached to some mangers.

The eggs referred to in the Old Testament were those of wild birds, whilst those in the New Testament were ordinary hens' eggs.

The domestic fowl of to-day is a native of India, and is not mentioned in the Old Testament. It was known in Palestine at the Christian era, and is supposed to have been introduced by the Romans into the countries they subjugated. They were common in Greece.

Egg hatching in Egypt is conducted largely by the Copts, an ancient Egyptian race. For such purposes they use a building containing 12 or 24 ovens, holding 150,000 eggs.

The proprietor of an oven collects the eggs from the peasants in the vicinity. The eggs are placed on mats strewn with bran, and are changed to positions nearer to, or further from, the heat, till the expiration of six days, four more days in the warmest position, and five days in a closed chamber. They are frequently changed during the next 5 days, outside air being carefully excluded.

The ancient Egyptian incubators are mentioned by Aristotle, Deodorus, and others.

Bounewain's incubator, invented in 1777, was heated by hot water. Tubes run back and forth through the machine containing the hot water, above which the eggs are placed.

In the year 1831 there were 105 of these establishments in Lower Egypt using 19,000,000 eggs, of which 13,000,000 produced chickens, thus saving the valuable time of 1,500,000 hens for three weeks of inactivity and several succeeding weeks of care of their broods.

Poultry raising may be classed as one of the accompaniments of a stock farm. The raising of chickens, in particular, has become an important industry, and modern science has contributed no little to the increase in the number of chickens annually hatched.

More modern inventors use various methods of heating.

The following table shows the length of time required for hatching eggs: Swan, 42 days; goose, 35 days; turkey, 28 days; peafowl, 28 days; duck, 28 days; common hen, 21 days; pigeon, 14 days; canary birds, 14 days.

Hen's eggs are hatched by being kept at a temperature of 104° for three weeks.

It is estimated that 50,000,000 eggs are consumed daily in the United States.

456,910,916 dozens of eggs were produced in the United States in the year 1880.

CARE OF STOCK

1. Feeder.
2. Salt Feeder.
3. Grooming.
4. Hen's Nest.
5. Egyptian Incubator.
6. U. S. Patent, Sheep Rack—A. D. 1881.
7. U. S. Patent, Manger—A. D. 1882.
8. U. S. Patent, Grooming—A. D. 1882.
9. U. S. Patent, Salt Feeder—A. D. 1883.
10. U. S. Patent, Incubator—A. D. 1883.
11. U. S. Patent, Horse Brush—A. D. 1884.
12. U. S. Patent, Fodder Cutter—A. D. 1884.

1

2

3

4

5

6

7

8

9

10

11

12

SLAUGHTERING AND MEAT CUTTING

IN the sculptures at Thebes butchers are represented sharpening their knives on a round bar of metal, which is suspended from their girdles or from the hem of the apron. This was evidently a steel.

The daily provision of meat for King Solomon's household was ten fat oxen and twenty oxen from the pasture.

The Romans established regular colleges, or companies, composed of a certain number of citizens, whose office was to furnish the city with the necessary cattle, and to superintend the butchers in preparing and vending the meat.

Nero built a noble market for the sale of butchers' meat.

Butchers' sheds, for the sale of meat, were first erected at Dunstable, England, in 1279.

In the middle ages the right of a common slaughter house, where the inhabitants might have their beasts killed, was a feudal privilege.

The old plan of making sausage was to cut the meat by means of cleavers, one in each hand. In early times, in the West, sausage was cut on the block by an axe. This was much slower than the handy little pair of cleavers, which were kept for the purpose and went the round of a settlement when hog butchering began.

The earlier forms of sausage machines used cleavers, which were at first on levers tripped by cam movement from the main shaft.

Afterward knives were made to reciprocate vertically by means of crank and shaft. The tub usually rotates beneath the knives so as to bring the meat in succession beneath the cutters. A scraper lifts the meat and turns it over so that the knives shall not repeat the blow in the same place.

The favorite domestic form of sausage cutter is a compact little machine. It is either a spiral row of steels, projecting radially from a barrel and forcing the meat between knives projecting inwardly from the casing; or, it has a series of radial knives on each of a pair of cylinders, placed so as to make a shear cut against each other; or the single barrel has knives which cut against opposed edges inside the case.

In each case the spiral vane forces the meat through the machine, which is cut as it passes along, and is discharged at the end opposite that at which it was fed.

Slaughtering apparatus for beeves usually consists of a mode of hauling the animal up to the place where it is stunned by a pole axe, and then bled. Also of a hoisting tackle, by which it is lifted while the skin and viscera are removed, and then swung clear of the floor to be washed and left to cool.

The slaughter of cattle in the United States per year is estimated at 8,500,000 head, and of hogs at 4,500,000.

One of the great industries connected with the supply of food, viz., slaughtering and meat packing, yields an aggregate product of 303,562,413 pounds per year in the United States.

SLAUGHTERING AND MEAT CUTTING

1. Primitive Scalding.
2. English, Catching and Suspending—A.D. 1808.
3. U. S. Patent, Meat Chopper—A. D. 1874.
4. U. S. Patent, Catching and Suspending—A. D. 1881.
5. U. S. Patent, Meat Slicer—A. D. 1881.
6. U. S. Patent, Scalding—A. D. 1882.
7. U. S. Patent, Catching and Suspending—A. D. 1882.
8. U. S. Patent, Scalding and Scraping—A. D. 1882.
9. U. S. Patent, Cutting and Mincing—A. D. 1883.

SLAUGHTERING AND MEAT CUTTING

872 Slaughtering and Meat Packing Establishments in the United States

	1870	1880
Capital Invested, ..	$22,124,787.00	$49,419,213.00
Value of Productions, ...	62,140,439.00	303,562,413.00
Wages Paid, ...	2,007,101.00	10,508,530.00
Hands Employed,..	6,485	27,297

401 Patents Granted by the United States

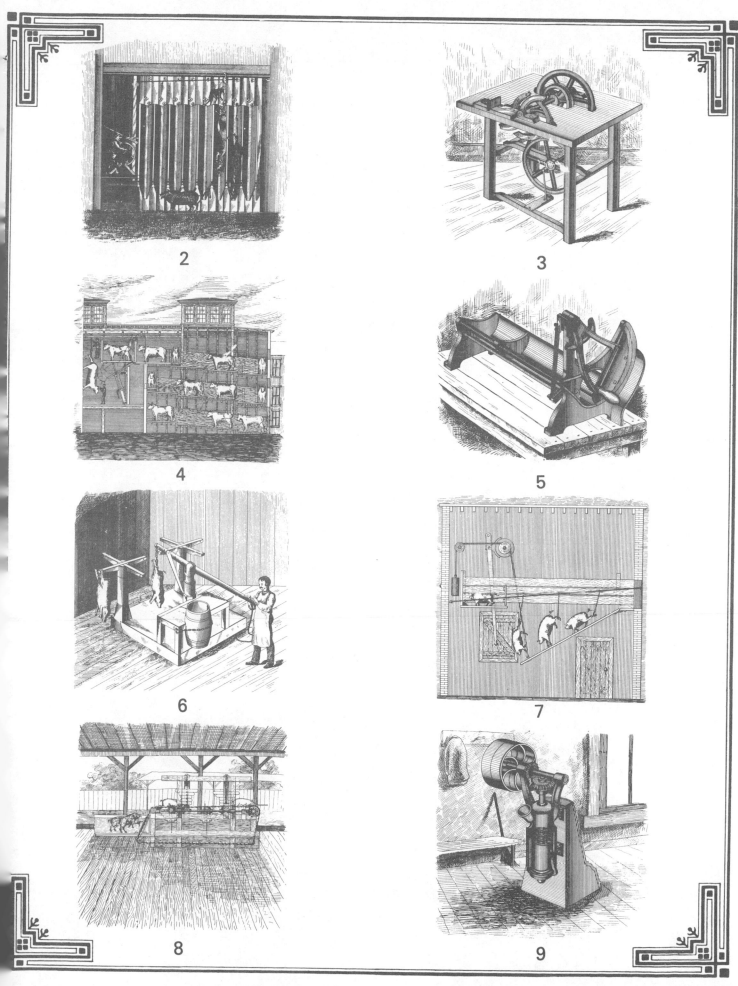

2

3

4

5

6

7

8

9

CREAMERY AND MILK

THE Liban (coagulated milk) of the Arabs was the usual form in which milk was, and is, used in Arabia.

The Turks show their Tartar origin in their preference for sour milk.

The Arabians and Turks have a preparation of curdled milk called "clan" by the former, and "yaourt" by the latter, which they preserve in bags. Fresh yaourt is much used by the Turks, and Europeans soon acquire a taste for it.

In olden times one or more cows were kept for general use of a village.

Houses for the protection of cows were not in general use until the 13th century.

CREAMERY AND MILK

3,932 Cheese and Butter Factories
in the United States

	*1860	1880
Capital Invested, ..	$8,000.00	$9,604,803.00
Value of Productions, ...	13,400.00	25,742,510.00
Wages Paid, ...	984.00	1,546,495.00
Hands Employed,..	7	7,903

*Cheese only

FARM DAIRY PRODUCTS

	1860	1880
Milk sold or sent to factories, galls, ...	Not reported	530,129,755
Butter made, pounds, .	459,681,372	777,250,287
Cheese made, pounds,	103,663,927	27,272,489

	Primitive Mode	Present Machine
CAPACITY— Time required to separate cream and milk,.......	24 hrs.	13 mins.
Loss by imperfect separation, ...	1/2	0
Gallons Milk separated per hour, ...		120

460 Patents Granted by the United States

A writer says that it was the common opinion in the Virginia Colony "that housing and milking cows in winter would kill them."

Fresh milk, in Uruguay, is sold by driving cows from door to door along the streets, and milking them into jars brought out by the customers.

At the works of the Aylesbury Condensed Milk Co. in England, 200 persons are employed, and the milk of 1,200 cows is daily evaporated.

Borden's American process of condensing milk is protected by letters patent.

There are a number of factories for condensing milk about New York City, where it is sold from house to house fresh from the condensing vats. Thousands of gallons of milk are daily prepared to supply the demand in the Army and Navy, and for foreign consumption.

Colvin's Hydraulic Cow Milker combines a cattle stall and compound milking apparatus operated by power; it is said that three machines are sufficient to milk 60 cows in the time it would take six men to milk them by hand.

It requires 15,000,000 cows to supply the demand for milk and its products in the United States.

The value of the butter, cheese, and milk produced in the United States in the single year of 1884 was $500,000,000, and the value of dairy products aggregated something like $100,000,000 more than the entire wheat crop of the country was worth.

CREAMERY AND MILK

1. Primitive Hand Milker.
2. Primitive Dairy.
3. Primitive Dutch Deep Setting Creamer.
4. U. S. Patent, Vacuum Milker—A. D. 1868.
5. U. S. Patent, Aerating Creamer—A. D. 1872.
6. U. S. Patent, Centrifugal Creamer—A.D. 1872.
7. U. S. Patent, Water Sealed Can—A.D. 1879.
8. U. S. Patent, Cabinet Creamer—A. D. 1879.
9. U. S. Patent, Elevator Creamer—A.D. 1880.
10. U. S. Patent, Centrifugal Creamer—A. D. 1881.
11. U. S. Patent, Vacuum Creamer—A. D. 1883.
12. U. S. Patent, Vacuum Milker—A. D. 1883.

1

2

3

4

5

6

7

8

9

10

11

12

CHURNS

THE ancient method of making butter was probably the same as that practiced by the Bedouin Arabs and the Moors at the present day, the cream being placed in a goat skin and agitated by hand or treading upon it with the feet.

The butter and honey mentioned by Isaiah vii, 15, is to this day an article of food in the East. The butter and honey are mixed, and the bread dipped therein.

It was butter of kine and milk of sheep that made Jeshurine "wax fat."

Abraham took butter and milk, and the calf which he had dressed, and set them before three stranger visitors.

Sisera asked water, and Jael, the wife of Heber the Kennite, gave him milk. She brought forth buttter in a lordly dish before she nailed him to the ground with a tent pin and hammer.

Job refers to the time when he annointed his feet, or, as he expressed it, "washed my steps with butter, and the rock poured me out oil. Surely the churning of milk bringeth forth butter."

The oldest mention of butter is the account given of the Scythians, by Herodotus: "These people pour the milk of their mares into wooden vessels, cause it to be violently stirred or shaken by their blind slaves, and separate the part that rises to the surface, as they consider it more valuable than that which is collected below it."

At the present time, in Uruguay, South America, the dairyman pours the milk, while still warm, into an inflated pig or goat skin, hitches it to his saddle, and gallops five or six miles into town, with the milk sack pounding along on the road behind him. When he reaches his destination his churning is over, the butter is made, and he peddles it from door to door.

Churns are classified in the United States Patent Office as follows: Double acting, reciprocating, multiple dasher, single dasher, combined lever and crank mechanism, food mechanism, hand and foot mechanism, rocking seat mechanism, diagonal dasher, horizontal single dasher, horizontal double dasher, concentric shafts, parallel shafts, vertical, &c.

The motion which is said to give the best results in churning is that which produces a thud or shock. The swing churn is a small keg or slender barrel, suspended in a horizontal position, for making small quantities of butter. It has been highly recommended. Various wheel churns have been invented.

From 40 to 60 minutes is the recognized time in which to make butter.

The census of 1880 estimated the production of butter in the United States as 806,672,071 pounds annually.

CHURNS

1. Primitive Scythian.
2. Primitive Grecian.
3. Dutch Mode of Operating.
4. Plunger.
5. U. S. Patent, Rotary—A. D. 1807.
6. U. S. Patent, Vibrating—A. D. 1808.
7. U. S. Patent, Working Body—A. D. 1835.
8. U. S. Patent, Working Body—A. D. 1835.
9. U. S. Patent, Working Body—A. D. 1872.
10. U. S. Patent, Rotary—A. D. 1883.
11. U. S. Patent, Vibrating—A. D. 1884.
12. U. S. Patent, Rotary—A. D. 1884.

CHURNS

3,932 Cheese and Butter Factories in the United States

	*1860	1880
Capital Invested, ..	$8,000.00	$9,604,803.00
Value of Productions, ...	13,400.00	25,742,510.00
Wages Paid, ...	984.00	1,546,495.00
Hands Employed,..	7	7,903

*Cheese only.

CAPACITY—	Primitive Mode	Present Machine
Pounds Butter per day, ...	20	1,500
Hands Employed per day, ...	1	1

1,776 Patents Granted by the United States

1

2

3

4

5

6

7

8

9

10

11

12

EGG CARRIERS

THE largest eggs of which we have any account were found in 1850, in Madagascar. They belonged to a bird which has become extinct. Two of these eggs are preserved in the French Academy; one of them measures 13¼ inches in its largest diameter and 8½ in the shortest; the shell is about one-eighth of an inch thick; the capacity of the egg is about 8½ quarts. The size of the boxes necessary to carry this size of eggs could hardly be considered.

The immense increase in the hens' egg industry of late years has made a convenient method of transporting them a necessity. In 1880 the number of eggs reported was 456,910,916 dozens. This number has been steadily increased.

Many devices have been patented for the convenience of the consumer and the tradesman. One of these is the egg assorter, by which eggs are assorted according to quality, being so placed that a strong light is brought to bear upon them when stuck into holes in a board. Their comparative translucency is then observed, and is accepted as an evidence of quality.

Another apparatus, known as the egg detector, was invented for the same purpose. In this the eggs are placed upright in the holes in the lid of a dark chamber, and their transmitted light is observed upon a mirror. Their quality is determined by their translucency, as evinced by the relative transmission of light. An egg becomes opaque and cloudy as it becomes spoiled.

A simple appliance for holding eggs is a pair of tongs, not unlike sugar tongs, into which the wider part of an ordinary egg usually fits. There are two designs of an egg glass; one is for holding the egg while eating it, the other is a sand glass, which runs three minutes, the proper time for boiling an egg to render it more digestible.

Egg packers, transporting cases and carriers are in many varieties of shape, size and material. The most useful case for packing is a wooden box, divided into squares just large enough to hold one egg. These squares are made of thin brown pasteboard, and are packed in layers until the box is full.

In one invention frames are supplied with cloth pockets for carrying the eggs. This, however, is too expensive to be used on a large scale.

A primitive method, but one still practiced at the present time, is to pack eggs in a box with sawdust or salt, strewn in so as to prevent contact.

EGG CARRIERS

1. U. S. Patent, Egg Holder—A. D. 1855.
2. U. S. Patent, Egg Packer—A. D. 1865.
3. U. S. Patent, Egg Transporting Case—A. D. 1867.
4. U. S. Patent, Egg Carrier—A. D. 1868.
5. U. S. Patent, Egg Carrier—A. D. 1869.
6. U. S. Patent, Egg Carrier—A. D. 1871.
7. U. S. Patent, Egg Carrier—A. D. 1872.
8. U. S. Patent, Egg Carrier—A. D. 1876.
9. U. S. Patent, Egg Carrier Box—A.D. 1878.
10. U. S. Patent, Egg Carrier Pail—A. D. 1882.
11. U. S. Patent, Egg Carrier Pail—A. D. 1883.
12. U. S. Patent, Egg Carrier Pail—A. D. 1884.

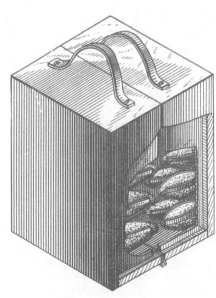

1

EGG CARRIERS

Eggs Produced in 1879, doz., ... 456,910,916

238 Patents Granted by the United States

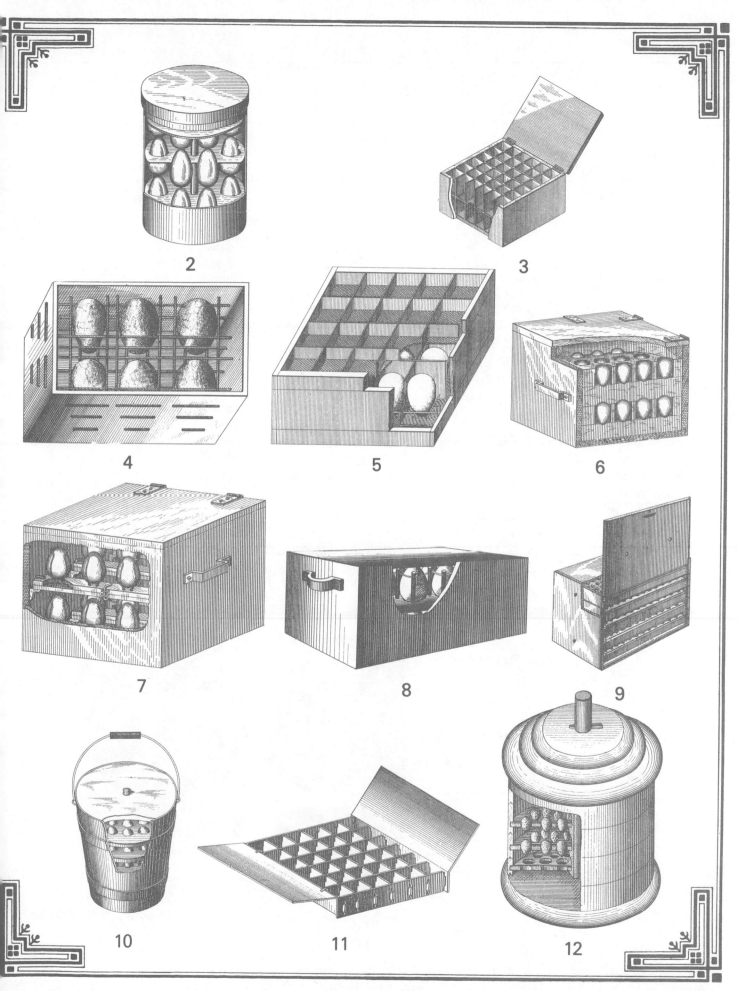

2

3

4

5

6

7

8

9

10

11

12

63

WINDMILLS

PAULO introduced windmills into Rome for grinding grain a little before the time of Augustus.

In the time of Hero, 150 B. C., organs were blown by the agency of a windmill, which worked the piston of an air pump.

They were used in England A. D. 1180, and from the twelfth to the fourteenth century notices of them are common.

Bartolomeo Verdi had a grant of land to build windmills, in Venice, in 1332.

In the twelfth century the Pope decided that the usufructs of water and windmills were taxable.

Those which turn wholly round are the most ancient.

The first mode adopted to present the vanes towards the wind was to float the mill and turn it in the water as occasion required.

The next was to put it on a post, and turn the building on this as an axis. This was called the German method. Then followed turning the cap or roof, which was a Dutch invention of the sixteenth century.

In 1772, Andrew Meikle, of Scotland, invented a plan for automatically adjusting the area of the sails to the force of the wind.

In 1804, Bywater, of England, patented a method of rolling up the sails to adjust them in like manner, by means of a weighted lever which was caused to operate gears connected by cords to cylinders on which the sails were wound.

The ball governor, from which Watt borrowed the idea, was first used in windmills.

In Holland windmills are employed in driving the scoop wheels which drain the polders.

Holland has over 12,000 windmills in operation, averaging eight horse power.

In many portions of the United States, especially in low countries where they have no water power, windmills are used for driving machinery, for thrashing and grinding grain, and for pumping water.

There are several large establishments in the United States for manufacturing machinery for windmills.

In the low lands along the Southern Atlantic coast windmills are used by the planters for driving the machinery of the rice and sugar mills.

WINDMILLS

1. Primitive—B. C. 150.
2. Horizontal Wheel—A. D. 1719.
3. U. S. Patent, Vertical Wheel—A. D. 1859.
4. U. S. Patent, Geared Vertical Wheel—A.D. 1873.
5. U. S. Patent, Hoisting—A. D. 1882.
6. U. S. Patent, Pumping Railroad Tank—A. D. 1883.
7. U. S. Patent, Farm—A. D. 1883.

WINDMILLS

69 Manufactories in the United States

	1860	1880
Capital Invested, ..	$8,550.00	$697,100.00
Value of Productions, ...	28,750.00	1,010,542.00
Wages Paid, ...	12,948.00	244,197.00
Hands Employed,..	27	596

	Present Machine
CAPACITY—	
Maximum gallons water pumped per day, ...	450,000
Hands employed per day, ...	1

908 Patents Granted by the United States

1

2

3

4

5

6

7

ARCHITECTURE

ARCHITECTURE is the art of inventing and drawing designs for buildings, or the science which teaches the method of constructing any edifice for use or ornament. It is divided into civil, military and naval.

Civil architecture was among the earliest inventions, and its works have been commonly regulated by some principles of hereditary imitation. Whatever rude structures the climate and materials of any country have obliged its early inhabitants to adopt for their temporary shelter have, with all their prominent features, been afterwards, in some measure, kept in view by their refined and opulent posterity.

The ancient colossal ruins abounding in Siam, Japan, the islands of the Indian Ocean, and the wonderful tombs, temples, and pyramids of Egypt proclaim the early knowledge of architecture.

To Greece we are indebted for the invention of the three principal orders—the Doric, Ionic and Corinthian—Rome added the Tuscan and the Composite. Each of these orders has a particular expression, so that a building may be solid, neat delicate or gay, according as the Tuscan, the Doric, the Ionic, the Corinthian or the Composite is employed.

The columns of the several orders are easily distinguishable by the ornaments that are peculiar to their capitals.

After the destruction of the Roman Empire the classic architecture of Greece and Rome was lost, but was revived by the Italians at the time of the restoration of letters. All the debased styles which sprang from vain attempts to imitate the ancients, and which flourished from the destruction of the Roman Empire till the introduction of the Gothic, have been united under one term, the Romanesque. The origin of the Gothic style is a matter of great uncertainty. The Saxon and Norman styles were so called because they were respectively used by the Saxons in England before the conquest, and by the Normans after it, in building their churches.

The Saxon and Norman continued to be the prevailing modes of building in England until the reign of Henry the Second, when the modern Gothic, or pointed style, was introduced.

In the fifteenth and sixteenth centuries Greek and Roman architecture were revived and brought the five classic orders again in use.

The following are the dates of the erection of a few celebrated edifices:

Pyramids, B. C. 1500; Solomon's Temple, B. C. 1004; Jupiter Capitolus, B. C. 616; Parthenon, B. C. 438; Pantheon, A. D. 13; Coliseum, A. D. 70; St. Sophia, A. D. 532; Mosque of Omar, A. D. 637; St. Peter's, Rome, A. D. 1616; St. Paul's, London, A. D. 1710.

The Gothic order gained ascendency in England in 1840, when it was adopted for the new houses of parliament.

The Bartholdi Statue of Liberty is in principle a duplicate of the Colossus of Rhodes. It is erected on Bedloe's Island, New York Harbor. The total height is 328 feet and 11 inches; the statue proper is 151 feet 2 inches.

The Washington Monument is the highest structure in the world, being 555 feet high.

ARCHITECTURE

1. Aboriginal Dwelling.
2. Primitive Door and Window.
3. Emigrant Cabin. Window.
4. U. S. Patent, Rolling Slat Shutter—A. D. 1835.
5. U. S. Patent, Rolling Slat Shutter—A. D. 1878.
6. U. S. Patent, Sliding Door—A. D. 1878.
7. U. S. Patent, Portable House—A. D. 1879.
8. U. S. Patent, Removable Window Sash—A. D. 1883.
9. Modern Villa.

ARCHITECTURE

9,184 Establishments in the United States

	1860	1880
Capital Invested, ..	$3,251,357.00	$19,441,358.00
Value of Productions, ...	12,646,392.00	94,152,139.00
Wages Paid, ...	3,868,672.00	24,582,077.00
Hands Employed,..	9,006	54,138

1,261 Patents Granted by the United States

1

2

3

4

5

6

7

8

9

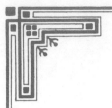
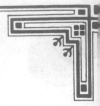

TYPES OF NAILS AND SPIKES

HARDLY any kind of hardware can boast of greater antiquity than nails, inasmuch as they are mentioned in the 4th chapter of the Book of Judges, and in other parts of the Bible.

The nails of ancient Egypt were of bronze.

NAILS AND SPIKES
62 Manufactories in the United States

	1860	1880
Capital Invested, ..	$5,810,250.00	$9,877,805.00
Value of		
Productions, ...	9,857,223.00	21,924,540.00
Wages Paid, ...	2,398,872.00	5,255,171.00
Hands Employed,..	6,878	8,910

117 Patents Granted by the United States

NAILS AND SPIKES

———

U. S. PATENTS
FROM
A. D. 1805
TO
A. D. 1884

There are about 300 varieties of nails in use, and ten sizes of each kind.

The term tenpenny, when applied to nails, is probably a corruption of pound, thus: a thousand fourpenny nails weigh four pounds, and one thousand tenpenny nails weigh ten pounds.

Nails are assorted: 1st, as to purpose used, as hurdle, pail, deck scupper, sheathing, fencing and slating; 2nd, form of the head, as rose, clasp, diamond, billed, clout and counter sink; 3d, form of points, as flat, sharp, spear and clinch; 4th, thickness, as fine, bastard, strong; 5th, sizes, as one-half to forty lbs.; 6th, material, as copper for sheathing ships, metal for roof coverings; 7th mode of manufacture, as wrought cut and cast.

Some nails are so small that 1,000 weigh only one and one-half ounces.

It is said that there are about 2,000 kinds of nails and rivets made and used for an almost infinite variety of purposes.

It is predicted that in the course of the next five years steel nails will have as completely supplanted iron nails as the steel rail has its iron predecessor. It is said that steel nails can be made cheaper than those of iron.

Spikes are nails larger than tenpenny, viz: 12-d are 3¼ inches long, 45 to pound; 16-d are 3¼ inches long, 28 to pound; 20-d are 4 inches long, 20 to pound; 30-d are 4¼ inches long, 16 to pound. Railway spikes are larger.

Spikes are known by shape, character, purpose, quality or size, as flat, narrow flat, wide flat, grooved, swelled, notched, barbed, forked, cylindrical, square, &c.

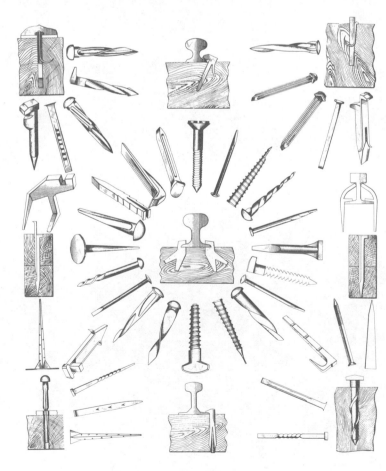

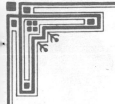

TYPES OF SCREWS

IN the year 1809 Ezra L'Hommedieu, of Connecticut, patented a double-podded screw auger, and in the same year informed the Secretary of the Treasury that "he made a machine for himself by which a man, aided by two boys, could make three hundred pounds per day of assorted screws, better than the imported ones, and that, in his opinion, in a short time the demands of the United States would be supplied by screws produced by his simple and cheap process."

Not only have improvements been made in machines for producing screws, but also in the shape and method of construction of the screw itself.

One of the chief improvements is the gimlet-pointed screw, which has almost superceded the old form of the screw ending in a blunt point.

It is singular that so simple an improvement as this, which is simply combining the screw point of the gimlet with the screw itself, should have been so recently made.

Screws and gimlets had both been long in use before the idea of combining them occurred to any one of the thousands daily engaged in the practical use of both, and this, too, when the gimlet itself was only a pointed screw.

In France gimlet-pointed screws were made over a hundred years ago, but, from the want of a simple change in the machinery used for making them, they did not possess the accuracy needed for bringing them into use.

Another late improvement in screws consists in the arrangement of the threads about the center cylinder. This differs from the ordinary screw in having three threads, which revolve about the core only once and a half in their passage from the top to the point, instead of having only one thread, which revolves many times in the same distance.

The advantage claimed of having the threads revolve at the angle is, that a screw so constructed can be driven in with a hammer instead of requiring the screw driver; also, that the threads are farther apart and take a stronger hold upon the wood, and hold with double the strength of an ordinary screw.

Some of the screws used in making watches at the Waltham Watch Manufactory are so minute as to seem like iron filings or grains of ground pepper.

A pound of steel, costing but fifty cents a pound, yields 100,000 of these screws, worth eleven dollars.

SCREWS
20 Manufactories in the United States

	1880
Capital Invested,	$4,265,000.00
Value of Productions,	2,184,532.00
Wages Paid,	456,542.00
Hands Employed,	1,585

98 Patents Granted by the United States

SCREWS

———

U.S. PATENTS
FROM
A. D. 1831
TO
A. D. 1884

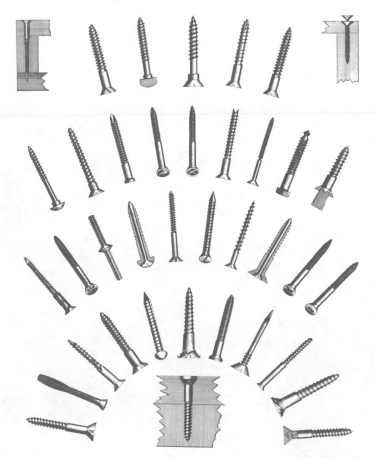

THE ancient Greeks and Romans warmed their houses by braziers, in which they used charcoal, and threw perfumes on the wood to correct any unpleasant effluvia. They also had a method of preparing wood to prevent smoking, which was by peeling off the bark and letting the wood lie a long time in water, and then drying it and likewise scorching it over the fire until it lost all moisture.

Stoves are of comparatively modern invention, and were probably first in use in the countries of the north of Europe. They were built of bricks and tiles of massive forms, and somewhat resembled ovens.

Dr. Franklin, who was one of the earliest writers on the subject, invented some very ingenious forms of stoves. His earliest inventions were made in 1745.

In 1771 Dr. Franklin completed and used in London a stove designed for burning bituminous coal, which consumed its own smoke.

Bonnemain appears to have been the first to introduce the circulation of hot water in a system of pipes as a means of warming apartments and buildings. He devised and put his plan in operation in 1777.

In Germany cast iron stoves are used to some extent.

Oliver Evans received, in 1800, the first United States patent for a "luminous stove" for burning the recently discovered hard Lehigh or stone coal.

The general introduction into the United States of grates and furnaces for burning anthracite coal did not commence until 1827.

The various methods which have been put into practice for producing a proper temperature in buildings may be reduced to the following: 1st, warming by fires placed in open chimney places; 2d, warming by flues under the floors or in walls; 3d, warming by close stoves of brick, earthenware or metal; 4th, warming by steam pipes; 5th, warming by hot water pipes; 6th, warming by heated air; 7th, warming by combinations of these methods.

Stoves in the United States are of the greatest diversity of forms. They are made of cast iron, of sheet iron, and sometimes of soapstone.

Stoves heated by jets of burning gas have been recently introduced.

HEATING

1. Primitive.
2. Benjamin Franklin's Stove—A. D. 1745.
3. U. S. Patent, Hot Air System—A. D. 1870.
4. U. S. Patent, Magazine Stove—A. D. 1875.
5. U. S. Patent, Magazine Stove and Warming Oven—A. D. 1880.
6. U. S. Patent, Steam Heating System—A. D. 1881.

HEATING

4,147 Patents Granted by the United States

1

2

3

4

5

6

STAND AND BRACKET LAMPS

THE most primitive lamps, were probably the skulls of animals, or certain sea shells, in which fat was burned.

Lamps were used in the early ages in China, India, Egypt, Greece and Rome, and preceded the use of candles.

Many beautiful forms of lamps have been taken from the excavations of Pompeii.

The Egyptians first used lamps in their temples.

Green porcelain lamps were found in the great pyramids of Ghizeh, and were also used in the tabernacle and the temples of the Jews.

The festival of Isis at Busirius was called "the feast of lamps." The lamps had wicks floating in oil which rested on salt water.

Hero wrote a description of a lamp, 150 B. C., in which a supply of oil from a reservoir below is driven up by means of air introduced into the base by an air pump. In another form the oil was raised by water introduced below the oil by means of a pipe.

The Argand lamp, which was introduced in 1786, was so named from its inventor, a native of Switzerland.

L. Augi, a Frenchman, invented the lamp chimney; he added it to the tubular neck and central air tube of Argand's lamp, and perfected the invention.

The introduction of the Argand lamp produced a revolution in the manufacture of lamps, but threatened with ruin all those whom the patent excluded from participating in the new trade, to such an extent that Argand was publicly persecuted by the tinners and iron mongers who disputed his rights to infringe the profits of their chartered vocation.

The streets of Boston, Mass., were lighted for the first time with lamps in 1774.

Sir Humphrey Davy invented, in 1815, the fine wire safety lamp, for preventing explosions by fire-damp in mines.

Lamps of present date are designated for purposes used, as bracket, car, cigar lighting, miners' and street; and form of construction, as forced draft, independent reservoir, safety tube, and central draft.

STAND AND BRACKET LAMPS

1. Primitive Greek and Roman.
2. Primitive Floating Light.
3. Primitive Argand—A. D. 1784.
4. Primitive Student Lamp.
5. Primitive Stand Lamp.
6. U. S. Patent, Carriage Lamp—A. D. 1865.
7. U. S. Patent, Bracket Lamp—A. D. 1874.
8. U. S. Patent, Automatic Cigar Lighting Lamp— A. D. 1879.
9. U. S. Patent, Safety Lamp—A. D. 1882.

STAND AND BRACKET LAMPS

74 Manufactories of Lamps and Lanterns in the United States

	1860	1880
Capital Invested, ..	$235,800.00	$1,873,625.00
Value of Productions, ...	578,020.00	3,357,829.00
Wages Paid, ...	135,848.00	742,423.00
Hands Employed,..	374	1,730

4,816 Patents Granted by the United States

1

2

3

4

5

6

7

8

9

SUSPENDED LAMPS

IT was customary among the Romans to have a lamp hanging from the ceiling. It was also the custom on occasions of national rejoicing to have public illuminations, when lamps were suspended at the windows of houses.

The streets of Antioch, according to St. Jerome, were provided with lamps.

In 1697 the streets of New York City were ordered "to be lighted." The lighting was to be done by a lantern suspended from a pole stretched out from the window of every seventh house.

An act of Parliament in 1736 was passed for the regular lighting of the streets of London, and an estimate was made of the expense of introducing small globular lamps. It was calculated that 4,300 would be required.

In 1783 the lighting of the streets of Baltimore, and a day police, were established by the town authorities. The essential parts of a lamp are a vessel containing liquid fat, from which a portion rises gradually by capillary attraction through the wick to the flame.

The introduction of mineral oils, known under the various names of paraffine, petroleum, kerosene, naphtha, &c., has, in a great measure, superseded the use of animal and vegetable oils for lighting purposes.

SUSPENDED LAMPS

1. Primitive Roman Chandelier.
2. Primitive Hall Lamp.
3. U. S. Patent, Suspended Lamp—A. D. 1875.
4. U. S. Patent, Suspended Lamp—A. D. 1875.
5. U. S. Patent, Suspended Chandelier—A. D. 1875.
6. U. S. Patent, Car Lamp—A. D. 1883.

SUSPENDED LAMPS

74 Manufactories of Lamps in the United States

	1860	1880
Capital Invested, ..	$235,800.00	$1,873,625.00
Value of Productions, ...	578,020.00	3,357,829.00
Wages Paid, ...	135,848.00	742,423.00
Hands Employed ..	374	1,730

4,816 Patents Granted by the United States

1

2

3

4

5

6

LANTERNS

PERHAPS the original lantern is to be found in some varieties of fire flies in which the phosphorescent light (like Alfred's lantern, A. D. 890) is protected by a horny covering.

The earliest example of a lantern is in sculpture at Alabastron, representing a patrol of soldiers armed with spears, shields and battle axes, preceded by one carrying a lantern a little in advance; the panels were probably of talc, the lapis specularius of the Romans.

The Egyptian lantern consisted of a waxed cloth strained over a cylinder of wire rings, with top and bottom of perforated copper.

Lanterns are referred to by Greek authors. Alexis said "The man who first invented the idea of walking out at night was very careful not to get his fingers burnt." Lanterns have been disinterred at Herculaneum and Pompeii. In the latter place one was found in the vestibule of a house beside a skeleton; the person was probably trying to escape in the thick darkness of the descending ashes.

The Roman lantern was made of bronze, with panes of bladder, horn, mica, parchment, and oiled silk.

The horn lantern of Alfred the Great had a graduated candle, which was his time measure.

Lanterns were used to some extent in London as early as 1417. It is recorded that "Lanthorns with lights bee hanged out on winter evenings betwist Hallowtide and Candlemas."

The Abbe, Laudati, in 1662, obtained the exclusive privilege of letting out portable lanterns in Paris.

During the sixteenth, seventeenth and eighteenth centuries various European cities adopted the practice of lighting the streets by fixed lanterns.

The Chinese have a festival called "the Feast of Lanterns," in which they make an extraordinary display of the greatest variety, some being of enormous size, sometimes twenty-five and thirty feet in diameter.

Lanterns for lighting streets have been superseded by gas and electric lights.

The use of lanterns is now restricted to hand, ships, mining, etc., where the introduction of pipes is not attainable.

LANTERNS

1. Primitive Egyptian.
2. Primitive Roman.
3. Primitive Square.
4. Primitive Globe.
5. Primitive Miner's Safety
6. U. S. Patent, Globe—A. D. 1884.
7. U. S. Patent, Miner's Safety—A. D. 1878.
8. U. S. Patent, Globe—A. D. 1878.
9. U. S. Patent, Globe—A. D. 1878.
10. U. S. Patent, Signal—A. D. 1879.
11. U. S. Patent, Globe—A. D. 1880.
12. U. S. Patent, Naphtha Gas—A. D. 1881.
13. U. S. Patent, Tubular—A. D. 1883.
14. U. S. Patent, Tubular—A. D. 1883.
15. U. S. Patent, Reflecting Globe—A. D. 1884.

LANTERNS

74 Manufactories in the United States

	1860	1880
Capital Invested, ..	$235,800.00	$1,873,625.00
Value of Productions, ...	578,020.00	3,357,829.00
Wages Paid, ...	135,848.00	742,423.00
Hands Employed,..	374	1,730

615 Patents Granted by the United States

1

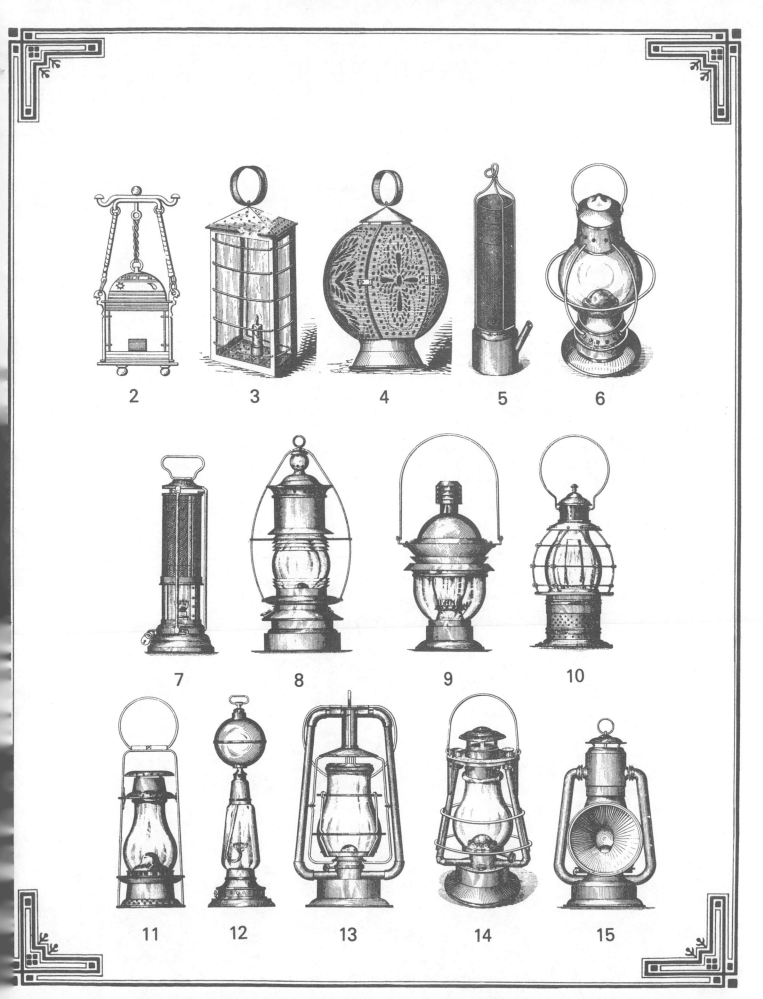

2 3 4 5 6

7 8 9 10

11 12 13 14 15

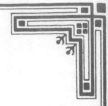

GAS BURNERS

DR. Clayton, in 1688, discovered that the air which comes from bituminous coal, when subjected to red heat in a retort, is inflammable and burns with a bright flame.

There is an account, published in 1733, of the carbonated hydrogen issuing from a coal work in Cumberland, England, having been collected in a bladder and made use of for the purpose of illumination, the gas being ignited at the extremity of a small tube attached to the bladder.

Mr. William Murdock, of Soho, England, in 1792, was the first person who put in practice the idea of producing light on an extensive scale by means of gas, and in 1798 applied it for the lighting of the very extensive manufactory of Messrs. Boulton, Watt & Co., at Soho, near Birmingham.

The illumination of the Soho Works by gas, in 1802, seems to have brought it into general notice.

In 1806 a Company was established for the purpose of conveying gas by means of pipes along the streets of London, so that they, as well as the houses, might be regularly supplied with it.

The first gas burner was called the cock spur jet, next the fish tail, next the bat wing, then the iron Argand, the Albert shadowless, and the improved Argand. They are now classified under the following heads: Argand, anti-extinguishing, compound, hydro oxygen, hydro carbon, incandescent, illuminating, laboratory, multiple, oxy-hydrogen, regenerative, revolving, &c.

GAS BURNERS
35 Manufactories in the United States

	1860	1880
Capital Invested, ..	$1,310,850.00	$3,248,400.00
Value of Productions, ...	2,255,900.00	4,329,656.00
Wages Paid, ...	570,804.00	1,469,287.00
Hands Employed,..	1,632	3,069

215 Patents Granted by the United States

GAS BURNERS

1. Bat Wing.
2. Argand.
3. U. S. Patent, Argand—A. D. 1868.
4. U. S. Patent, Self Regulating—A. D. 1875.
5. U. S. Patent, Vapor—A. D. 1878.
6. U. S. Patent, Enriching Attachment—A. D. 1881.
7. U. S. Patent, Flat Flame—A. D. 1883.
8. U. S. Patent, Heating Attachment—A. D. 1883.
9. U. S. Patent, Automatic Cut-off—A. D. 1883.
10. U. S. Patent, Regenerative Chamber—A. D. 1883.
11. U. S. Patent, Illuminating Burner—A. D. 1884.
12. U. S. Patent, Electric Lighting—A. D. 1884.

1

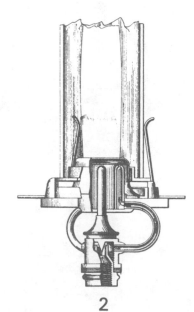

2

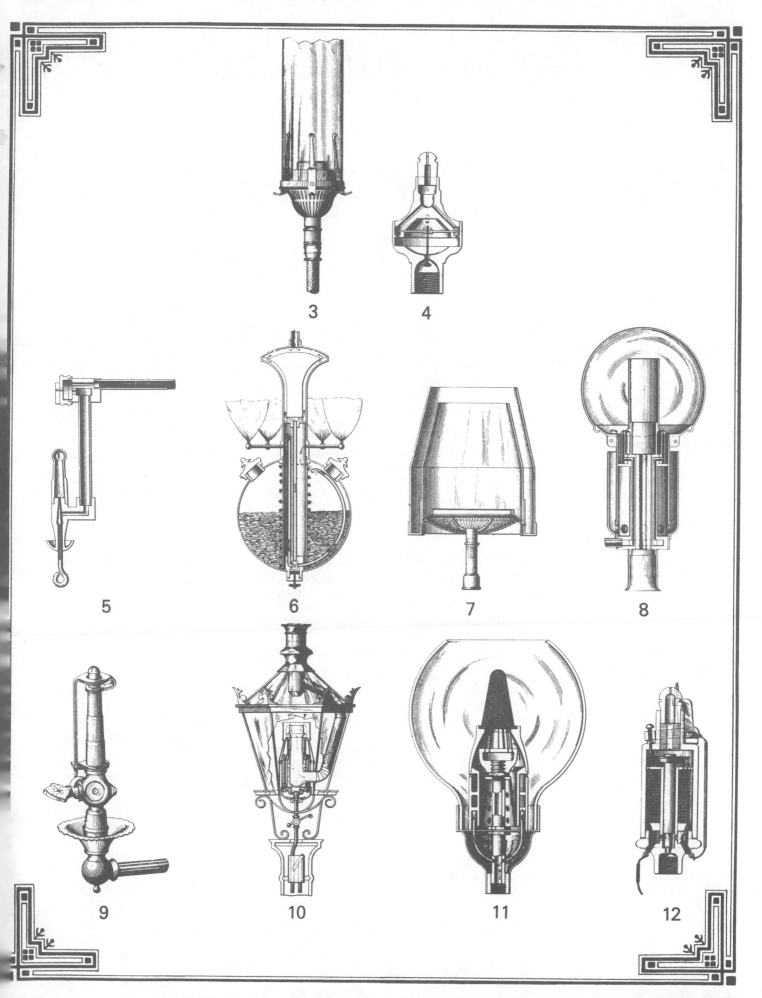

3

4

5

6

7

8

9

10

11

12

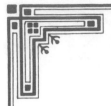

ELECTRIC ILLUMINATION
AND MOTORS

ELECTRICITY is derived from the Greek *elektron,* meaning amber, that being the first substance in which the existence of an electric fluid capable of being excited and accumulated was observed by Thales, of Miletus, in 600 B. C.

Electricity as a science, however, was first written of by William Gilbert, a London physician, A. D. 1600.

Boyle, about 1670, discovered that a diamond became electrical, and emitted light in a dark room, when friction was applied to it; and Hawkshaw, in 1709, discovered the electrical properties of glass.

The first electrical machine was made by Otto de Guerricke, of Magdeburgh, in 1660. It was a globe of sulphur, but glass cylinders were soon found to be more powerful.

Up to 1750, however, the friction was applied by the dry hand of the experimenter, until the cushion and silk floss were invented by Winckler, of Leipsic.

Metallic conductors originated with Stephen Gray in 1734, and though the accumulation of electric power in coated jars was discovered in 1745 by M. Von Kleist, Dean of the Cathedral in Corunna, the subsequent experiments of Cuneus, of Leyden, have been preserved in the Leyden jar.

The electrical battery was discovered by Gralable, a German electrician.

Electricity was first applied to medical purposes by Kratzenstein, at Halle, in 1744.

ELECTRIC ILLUMINATION
AND MOTORS

Denoting the cost of Electric Arc Light of the
intensity of one standard candle by 1.0
The cost of wax candles of the same intensity is ...75.0
The cost of stearin candles of the
    same intensity is 55.0
The cost of oil candles of the
    same intensity is 16.0
The cost of gas candles of the
    same intensity is 8.5

1,366 Patents Granted by the United States

In 1752 Franklin demonstrated the identity of lightning with the electric spark, and drew electricity from the clouds.

The first patents for electricity in the U. S. Patent Office were issued to D. Harrington, of Philadelphia, in 1833, '34, and '35, to cure disease.

The electric light was first brought into notice in this country by Greener & Straite, who took out a patent in 1846 for a light generated by the combustion of two carbon points.

The magneto-electric light was first applied for illuminating purposes at the lighthouse at Dungeness, England, in 1862, and was introduced at La Héve, France, a year or two later.

In this country the first patent for a dynamo was issued to Moses G. Farmer in 1875, which was similar in its construction to the series wound reactionary dynamos now found in general use.

Brush, with his dynamo and improvements upon arc lamps, came two years later.

The first patent for an improvement in the arc light was granted to Collier & Baker in May, 1858. It consisted of two electrodes of carbon; the upper carbon was prevented from contact with the lower by a retaining diaphragm of metal, through which a point projected. It acted by a mecurial feed, the carbons being forced forward by the mercury in which they were immersed. As a practical lamp, it was not a success.

The electric light may be said to have been in general use in this country since 1878.

In 1838 Jacobs propelled a small shallop on the river Neva, near St. Petersburg, in Russia, at the rate of four miles an hour, three miles against the stream. He had four fixed electro-magnets, and the same number of revolving ones, to which the axle that carried the paddle wheels was attached. His battery, consisting of sixty-four pairs of platinum plates, each presenting a surface of thirty-six square inches, was charged with nitric and sulphuric acid on Grove's plan.

In 1849 Prof. Page propelled a car on the tracks of the Baltimore and Ohio Railroad from Washington to Bladensburg—a distance of six miles—at the rate of nineteen miles an hour.

The patent for the Page motor was granted January 21, 1854. In this motor the two armatures consist of long cores of wire, which are adapted to slide with an oscillatory motion through two pairs of solenoids, made up of successive sections, which are brought into action by sliding commutators actuated by rods from eccentrics on the fly wheel shaft, being entirely analogous to the cut-off mechanism used in a steam engine.

The use of electricity as a motor is not general, as it has not yet been sufficiently demonstrated that it is cheaper than coal.

Prof. Ayrton, however, states that the cost of coal for producing power is L790,000 a year in Sheffield alone, and that electricity can supply this want; and according to Sir William Thomson, the source of power by this means would be 133 times as cheap.

ELECTRIC ILLUMINATION
AND MOTORS

1. Electric Lighting—A. D. 1813.
2. Electric Motor—A. D. 1838.
3. U. S. Patent, Incandescent Lamps—A. D. {1848. 1873. 1878.
4. U. S. Patent, Magneto Machine and Arc Light—A. D. 1850.
5. U. S. Patent, Magneto Machine and Arc Light—A. D. 1871.
6. U. S. Patent, Magneto Generator & Electric Candle—A. D. 1877.
7. Electric Railway—A. D. 1880.
8. Dynamo—A. D. 1883.
9. Transmitting Energy from Distant Sources of Power for Lighting, etc.—A. D. 1883.

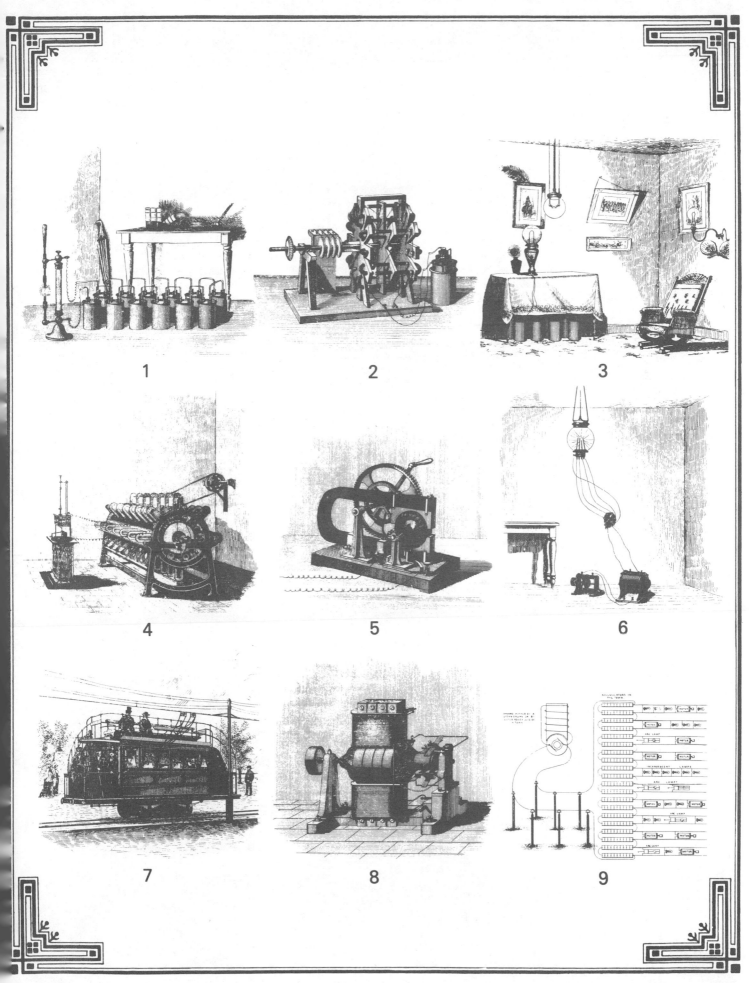

1

2

3

4

5

6

7

8

9

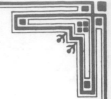

TELEPHONES

THIS is from two Greek words—*telos,* far distant, and *phones,* sound.

The instruments by which articulate sound is now conveyed were invented by Alexander Graham Bell, of Boston, to whom a patent was granted March 7, 1876, for a speaking telephone. This gentleman had been studying the subject of conveying sound over an electric wire since 1867. His experiments were patiently conducted for nine years, often under discouraging circumstances; but he was rewarded in the end, and is one of the few inventors who has reaped large pecuniary returns from his invention.

The first public exhibition of the telephone was at the Centennial exhibition in Philadelphia in July, 1876. The first lines for general use were erected in the early part of 1877.

The telephone was found to be incomplete without some means of calling the person at the other end of a distant line. Various kinds of call bells were tried and failed, and many inventions made before the magneto-bell, which is now in general use, was devised.

Patents were granted for transmitters to E. Berliner, Thomas A. Edison, and Francis Blake. All these were on the same general principle, but the Blake transmitter is the one generally used.

Single lines connecting two or three persons were soon found to be of limited value, and exchanges were organized, composed of subscribers, all of whom had lines running to a central office, so that any subscriber could communicate with any other subscriber to the exchange through the central office.

The first exchanges were started early in the year 1878, and at about the same time, in Chicago and New Haven.

Many inventions of great value have been made in switch boards and other machinery for the central office.

The telephone was early introduced into England and on the continent of Europe, and is now in use in every part of the civilized world.

No invention was ever made which came into such general and universal use so rapidly as the telephone.

TELEPHONES

1. Primitive.
2. Musical.
3. U. S. Patent, Magneto—A. D. 1876.
4. U. S. Patent, Electrical Exchange System—A. D. 1879.
6. U. S. Patent, Radiophone—A. D. 1880.

TELEPHONES

Number in use in the United States	376,691
Number Manufactured,	584,104
Number Exported,	98,015
Total Number in Use,	477,344

1,472 Patents Granted by the United States

1

2

3

4

5

6

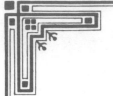

TELEGRAPHY

THIS is from two Greek words, *telos,* far distant, and *graphein,* to write.

The first patent granted for a telegraph in the United States was to J. Grant, of Massachusetts, in 1800.

The first telegraph erected in this country was on Long Island, by Harrison Gray Dyer, who used practical electricity, and dyed marks on chemically-prepared paper by means of electric sparks.

Although Prof. Morse is generally considered to be the father of the telegraph, as a matter of fact, Messrs. Wheatstone & Cook, of England, obtained a patent for their electro-magnetic telegraph on the 10th June, 1840, while Prof. Morse's patent followed only ten days later. The Wheatstone & Cook apparatus was cumbersome, and never found a place among the practical inventions of the art in this country. It was, primarily, to Morse's apparatus, based upon his code of signaling and the use of a single line wire with his well-known recorder, that we owe success in telegraphy.

The first line of telegraph erected by Morse was in 1844, between Baltimore and Washington, which consisted of 40 miles of line and no wires.

Prof. Morse's invention consisted of a copper wire, insulated by means of a hempen strand, coated with tar pitch and India rubber. Morse could never have proved the utility of his invention if he had not had a patent to sell in shares to secure aid in introducing it.

The first patent for a printing telegraph was issued to Royal E. House in 1846, and this was the parent of a large class of inventions known as printing telegraphs, among which may be mentioned the Eain automatic telegraph, which was designed to avoid the Morse patent, and which resulted in a long litigation.

In April, 1868, Prof. Page obtained a patent, which was afterward, in 1871, reissued to his assigners, the Western Union Telegraph Company, in such broad terms as to include all telegraphic apparatus when a main circuit is caused to operate or control a local circuit, and also the use of a retractile spring to an armature of an electro-magnet. It consisted of a well-known form of induction apparatus, with an automatic circuit breaker, and was invented by Prof. Page many years before he took a patent, which was granted by special act of Congress, he being an employee in the Patent Office, and, therefore, disqualified by law to take an interest in any United States patent, except by inheritance or bequest.

In 1848 there were 2,000 miles of line and 3,000 miles of wire. In 1860 there were 17,582 miles of line and 26,375 miles of wire. In 1870, 53,403 miles of line and 107,245 miles of wire, and in 1880, 142,364 miles of line and 350,018 miles of wire.

These figures give some idea of the rapid progress of the telegraph in the United States.

In 1880 50,000,000 messages were sent, and the various companies employed 24,000 persons, and had 14,000 offices.

TELEGRAPHY

1. Indian Signal.
2. Franklin's Experiment—A. D. 1752.
3. Semaphore Signal—A. D. 1776.
4. Electric Telegraph—A. D. 1809.
5. U. S. Patent, Electro Magnetic Telegraph—A. D. 1840.
6. U. S. Patent, Quadruplex Telegraph—A. D. 1884.

TELEGRAPHY
1880

No. of Offices or Stations, ... 12,510
Miles of Line in Operation, ... 110,727
Miles of Wire in Operation 291,213
No. Messages Transmitted
  during the year, ... 31,703,181
No. Hands Employed, ... 14,928
Wages Paid, ... $4,886,128.00

1,006 Patents Granted by the United States

1

2

3

4

5

6

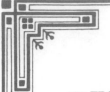

BEDSTEADS

BEDSTEADS were common in Egypt, and among the later Greeks.

They were only used by the wealthy classes; many ornate bedsteads are represented in the tombs at various points along the Nile.

The iron bedstead of King Og, of Bashan, who is said to have lived before the flood, was nine cubits long and four broad.

The bedsteads of the Greeks had four rails, legs, straps to support the mattress, a head board, and sometimes a footboard.

They were made of solid maple or box-wood; sometimes veneered with costlier wood, tortoise-shell or ivory, and sometimes had ornamental feet of silver. The mattress was of linen, woolen cloth, or leather, stuffed with straw or wool. Round and square pillows were used, and the covering consisted of soft woolen blankets and sheets.

The sleeping arrangements of the wealthy Greeks seem to have been good, but the Asiatics said "the Greeks do not know how to make a comfortable bed."

The Roman bedsteads were costly and beautiful. The weary climbed on them by stepladders, on the open side, the other side being closed by a sideboard. The beds were stuffed with wool or feathers, and had canopies, but no mention is made of curtains or testers.

The famous ancient bedstead of Ware, alluded to by Shakespeare, is still in existence. It is twelve feet square and was probably constructed A. D. 1500.

Many innovations and improvements have been made on the old-fashioned four-post bedstead which was provided with four high posts and tester, forming, with the curtains around it, a complete canopy by which the sleeper, if so disposed, could be fully protected against fresh air. It was formerly the practice to make the bed-bottom of coarse canvas having eyelet-holes along its edges, through which cord was passed, and thence over pins in the side, top and bottom rails, which supported the bed-bottom. This arrangement admitted of lacing the canvas as tightly as desired.

Various arrangements of slats and springs have superseded the old style and many improvements have been made in the manner of putting the posts together, so that the bedstead can be set up and taken down with great rapidity.

Invalid bedsteads are made with rising sections, so as to bring the body to a reclining or sitting posture.

Wardrobe, sofa, trunk, table and piano bedsteads are modes of concealing beds when not occupied, and also combine, with the bedstead, the other article of furniture which gives each its distinctive name.

Amongst the latest inventions is the hydrostatic, or water bed, used for medical purposes.

BEDSTEADS

1. Primitive.
2. Queen Anne.
3. English—A. D. 1772.
4. Wardrobe.
5. U. S. Patent, Sofa Bedstead—A. D. 1831.
6. U. S. Patent, Sofa Bedstead—A. D. 1860.
7. U. S. Patent, Combined Desk and Bedstead—A. D. 1871.
8. U. S. Patent, Bed Lounge—A. D. 1872.
9. U. S. Patent, Cabinet Bedstead—A. D. 1874.
10. U. S. Patent, Wardrobe Bedstead—A. D. 1876.
11. U. S. Patent, Wardrobe Bedstead—A. D. 1882.
12. U. S. Patent, Cot Settee—A. D. 1883.

FURNITURE
5,227 Manufactories in the United States

	1860	1880
Capital Invested, ..	$13,629,526.00	$44,946,128.00
Value of Productions, ...	25,632,293.00	77,845,725.00
Wages Paid, ...	8,909,998.00	23,695,080.00
Hands Employed ..	27,106	59,304

SUB CLASS
BEDSTEADS
3,345 Patents Granted by the United States

1

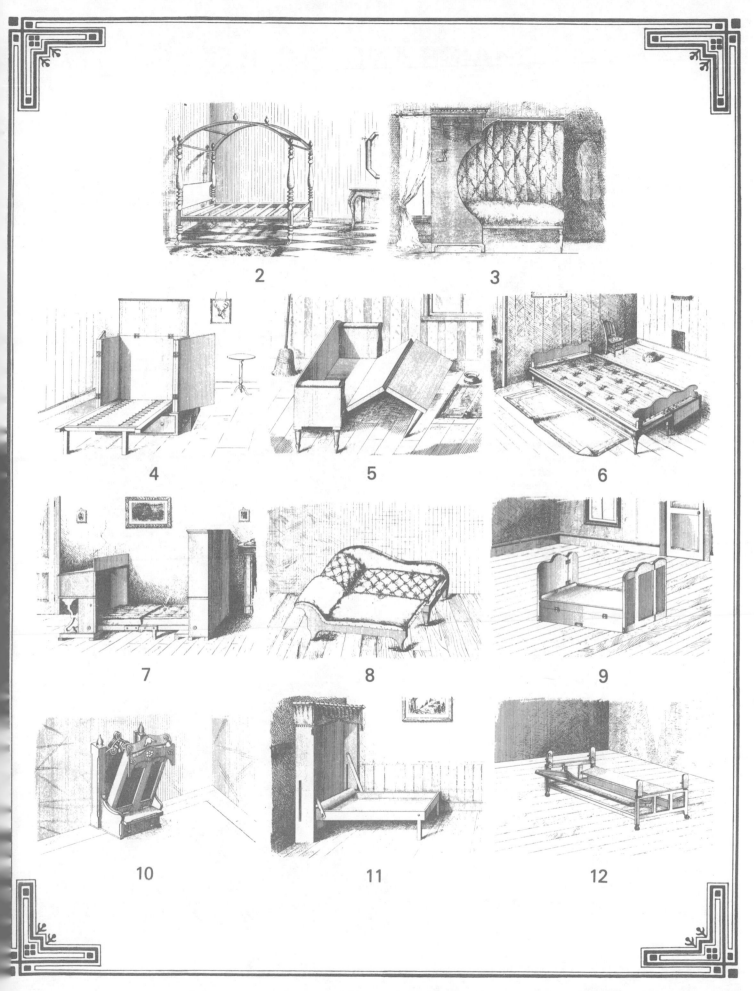

2

3

4

5

6

7

8

9

10

11

12

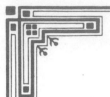

CHAIRS AND STOOLS

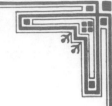

THE Egyptians were among the first to make chairs. On the tombs at Thebes are found representations of almost all the kinds of chairs which modern ingenuity has devised. Thrones, couches, sociables, folding, reclining, lazy back, leather seated, cane seated, split bottomed chairs, with curved backs, sides and legs with claw feed and food pads, and upholstered with gorgeous coverings.

The Egyptians, being an Asiatic race, it is presumable from the squatting posture in their paintings and bas reliefs, that the introduction of the chair came in the progress of refinement. The Egyptian chairs and stools were from 10¾ to 28 inches high.

Alexander gave a feast to 6,000 of his captains, and made them sit in chairs and couches of silver with purple covers.

Although chairs were not unknown to the Greeks and Romans, yet they seldom used them except on state occasions.

The curule chair was made of or adorned with ivory, and was introduced into Rome by Tarquin, from Viterbo, in Etruria. Two of them, made in the shape of our portable folding chairs, were discovered at Herculaneum.

The Anglo Saxons had rich curule chairs of state, similar to the Romans, and wooden and rush bottom chairs were common with them.

The sedan chair was first made use of by the Duke of Buckingham, in the reign of James I, to the great indignation of the people, who exclaimed that "he was employing his fellow creatures to do the work of beasts." A license for letting them out was granted Sir Saunders Duncomb, in 1634.

Modern chairs are classified under the following heads; Barber's, convertible, dentist's, folding, invalid, nursery, opera, oscillating, reclining, revolving, rocking, step ladder, surgical, and tilting.

CHAIRS AND STOOLS
384 Chair Manufactories in the United States

	1880
Capital Invested,	$6,276,364.00
Value of Productions,	9,807,823.00
Wages Paid,	3,311,286.00
Hands Employed,	10,575

2,596 Patents Granted by the United States

CHAIRS AND STOOLS

1. Primitive Seat.
2. Primitive Stool.
3. Primitive Stool.
4. Primitive Chair.
5. Egyptian Stool.
6. Egyptian Chair.
7. Crude Rocker.
8. U. S. Patent, Rocker—A. D. 1840.
9. U. S. Patent, Opera Chair—A. D. 1865.
10. U. S. Patent, Rocker—A. D. 1868.
11. U. S. Patent, Rocker—A. D. 1884.
12. U. S. Patent, Folding Seat—A. D. 1884.

1

2

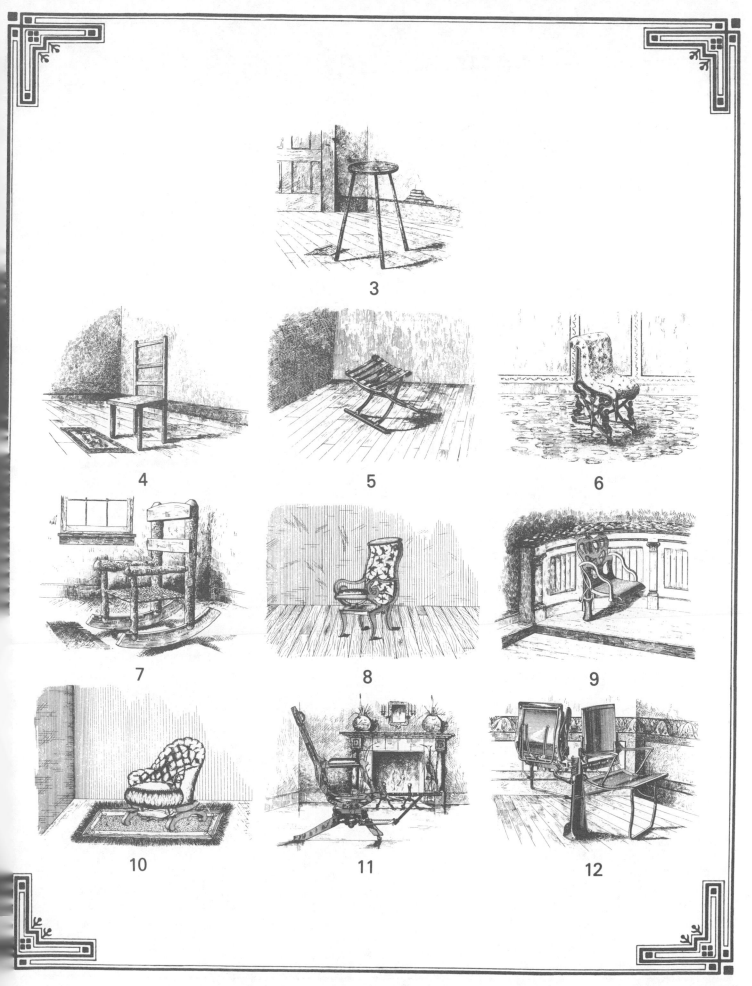

3

4

5

6

7

8

9

10

11

12

SCHOOL FURNITURE

ESKS, resembling those now in common use, have been discovered at Herculaneum, though the ancients usually wrote upon the knee, as is still customary in Asia and Africa.

Plato taught his scholars upon the Acropolis, in a grove of palm trees, standing himself, whilst the pupils stood, reclined upon the earth, or leaned against the numerous statues which adorned the grove and were the only "furniture" of this, the most magnificent school house either of ancient or modern times.

Fixed stone seats were provided in some of the ancient school houses. Then came movable wooden benches.

The Egyptian, who was taught to write on papyrus, was stretched prone upon the earthen or stone floor, resting upon his left arm or elbow, with the roll of papyrus also upon the floor within reach of his hand.

The Roman scholar, who learned to write upon parchment, reclined upon a bench, whilst the Hebrew sat up, with a table before him.

At the revival of literature, as light began to dawn from the night of the dark ages, schools were established where seats and tables were given to the pupils.

Seats and tables, or more latterly desks, are still the only form of school furniture. Modern times have required that these seats and desks should combine, as far as practicable, an easy and comfortable seat for the scholar, as great economy of space as is practicable, and durability.

The most common form is the seat composed of an iron frame and wooden seat, with a desk attached to the back, for the use of the scholars in the next rear row, with desk and seat both arranged to fold.

SCHOOL FURNITURE
2,257 Manufactories in the United States

	1860	1880
Capital Invested, ..	$13,629,526.00	$44,946,128.00
Value of Productions, ...	25,632,293.00	77,845,725.00
Wages Paid, ...	8,909. 998.00	23,695,080.00
Hands Employed,..	27,106	59,304

271 Patents Granted in the United States

SCHOOL FURNITURE
1. Primitive Bench.
2. Primitive Desk and Bench.
3. Primitive Seat and Desk.
4. U. S. Patent, Adjustable Seat—A. D. 1859.
5. U. S. Patent, Combined Seat and Desk—A. D. 1868.
6. U. S. Patent, Folding Desk and Seat—A. D. 1869.
7. U. S. Patent, Folding Desk and Seat—A. D. 1869.
8. U. S. Patent, Combined Desk and Seat—A. D. 1883.
9. U. S. Patent, Folding Desk and Seat—A. D. 1884.

1

2

3

4

5

6

7

8

9

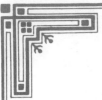

SATCHELS are of very ancient use. The name is from the Greek "Sakkos," and means a bag or sack.

Shakespeare writes of both a satchel and trunk.

A gripsack is something similar, and derives its name from the fact that it is generally carried in the hand.

Trunks were primarily rude wooden boxes for clothes or toilet articles. A covering of skin was added as their use became more general and travel more extended.

A very substantial trunk of the last century was made of horse skin tanned with the hair on. This was fastened on the box, with a flat or rounded top, with bright brass tacks, which were considered highly ornamental. These horse hair trunks were succeeded by leather trunks strapped with steel or wooden strips.

A cheap and portable trunk is a wooden box with curved lid covered with cloth and sometimes with paper in imitation of leather.

As early as 1596 the trunk-makers of France were incorporated into a company.

Roulston's trunk is one noted for its strength and durability. It has angle pieces to strengthen the corners, and guards to project from the corners of the body when shut. The corner longitudinal strips are bent at right angles at their ends to lap over vertical and transverse corner strips. The lower corner guards have projections for attachment and protection of the casters. The hinges are bent to lap around the ends of the trunk. A spring catch holds the lid case into the lid.

A Saratoga trunk was so named from the vast size it attained on account of the amount of clothing considered necessary for the person who frequented that favorite and fashionable resort, Saratoga Springs. This trunk attained huge proportions, and later inventions show it in the form of a folded wardrobe and bureau. Its compartments are many and various, and it is capable of holding without injury a great number of dresses and other articles of the toilet.

Trunks are made of wood, leather, paper, cloth, a preparation of zink and other materials.

The best trunk for ordinary land travel is one made of thick sole leather strapped with bands of the same material. No wood is used in the manufacture of this trunk, and it is capable of withstanding the roughest usage the average railway porter can administer. The best trunk for ocean travel is known as the steamer trunk, and is always bought by naval officers. This is perfectly flat on top, and is made of heavy sole leather, strapped with the same. It is made so as to fit squarely into its place and not roll about the other baggage.

Satchels and gripsacks are made of the same variety of material. Alligator skins are also coming into use for the manufacture of these useful articles.

TRUNKS

1. Primitive.
2. Japanese, 15th Century.
3. Gripsack.
4. U. S. Patent, Leather—A. D. 1836.
5. U. S. Patent, Bed—A. D. 1861.
6. U. S. Patent, Veneer—A. D. 1865.
7. U. S. Patent, Sheet Steel—A. D. 1871.
8. U. S. Patent, Bureau—A. D. 1871.
9. U. S. Patent, Saratoga—A. D. 1872.
10. U. S. Patent, Sole Leather—A. D. 1873.
11. U. S. Patent, Wardrobe—A. D. 1873.
12. U. S. Patent, Vulcanized Fiber—A. D. 1876.

TRUNKS

265 Establishments in the United States

	1860	1880
Capital Invested ...	$935,800.00	$2,792,256.00
Value of Productions, ...	2,836,969.00	7,252,470.00
Wages Paid, ...	692,572.00	1,786,586.00
Hands Employed,..	2,092	4,534

628 Patents Granted by the United States

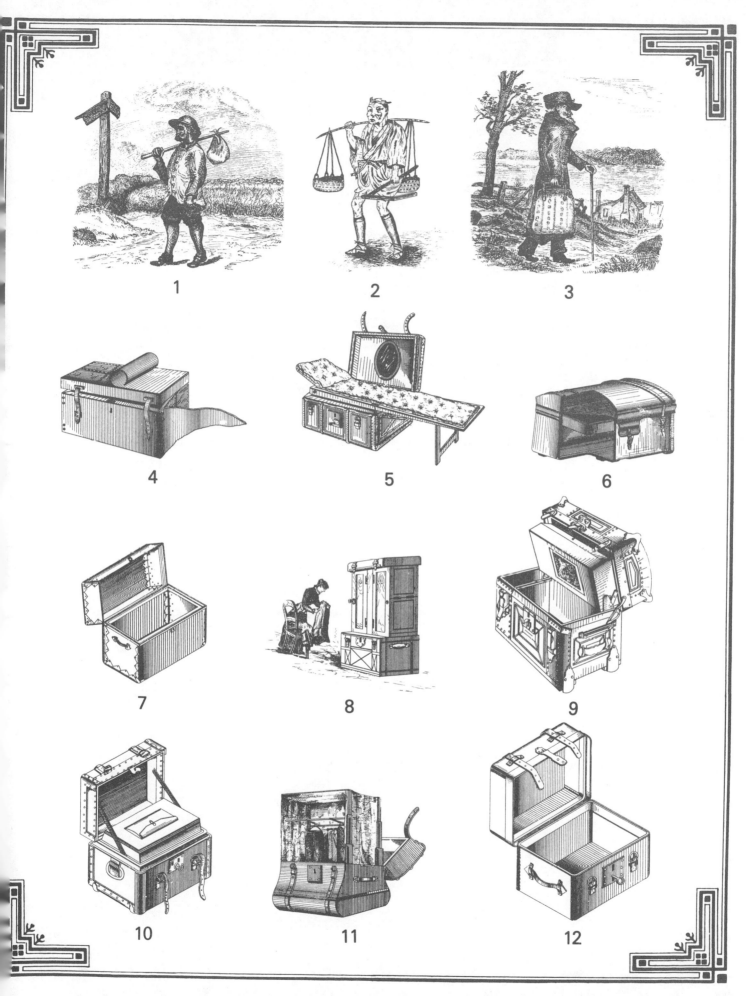

1

2

3

4

5

6

7

8

9

10

11

12

BANJOS AND GUITARS

THE banjo is a modern invention. It is much esteemed by the Negroes of the southern United States.

Its capacity is limited to the performance of simple tunes, and it is principally used for accompaniments.

The thrumming sound has a near resemblance to the Tam Tam of Africa and the Orient.

The guitar was known for more than fifteen centuries before the Christian era.

In the sculptures of Nimrod a musician is represented playing on a guitar.

Europeans derived it from Egypt through the intervention of the Saracens, after the lull of the dark ages, following the track through Spain.

The modern Arabs have an instrument which may be considered the Syrian guitar. The head is bent over, as in the European, the neck appears to be destitute of frets, the strings are seven, and made of catgut.

The guitar was introduced into England by Francis Corbeta, about 1660.

The guitar is the principal musical instrument of the Japanese. Their syanisie has three strings, two in the octave, the middle one giving the fifth.

The Spanish guitar has a hollow body with a round opening in the sounding board. The strings are six, and are stretched between a bar attached to the sounding board and the pegs, which are journaled in the head.

1. Ancient Citheras.
2. Spanish Guitar.
3. English Harp Lute—A. D. 1816.
4. U. S. Patent, Harp Guitar—A. D. 1831.
5. U. S. Patent, Pedal Guitar—A. D. 1873.
6. U. S. Patent, Banjo—A. D. 1876.
7. U. S. Patent, Guitar—A. D. 1881.
8. U. S. Patent, Zither—A. D. 1883.
9. U. S. Patent, Guitar Head—A. D. 1884.

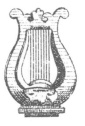
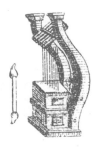

MUSICAL INSTRUMENTS
429 Manufactories in the United States

	1860	1880
Capital Invested, ..	$4,431,900.00	$14,446,765.00
Value of Productions, ...	6,548,432.00	19,254,739.00
Wages Paid, ...	2,378,520.00	7,098,794.00
Hands Employed,..	4,461	11,350

SUB CLASS
BANJOS AND GUITARS
84 Manufactories of Miscellaneous
Musical Instruments in the United States

Capital Invested,......................	$654,850.00
Value of Productions,...................	853,746.00
Wages Paid, ...	293,062.00
Hands Employed, ...	573

69 Patents Granted by the United States

1

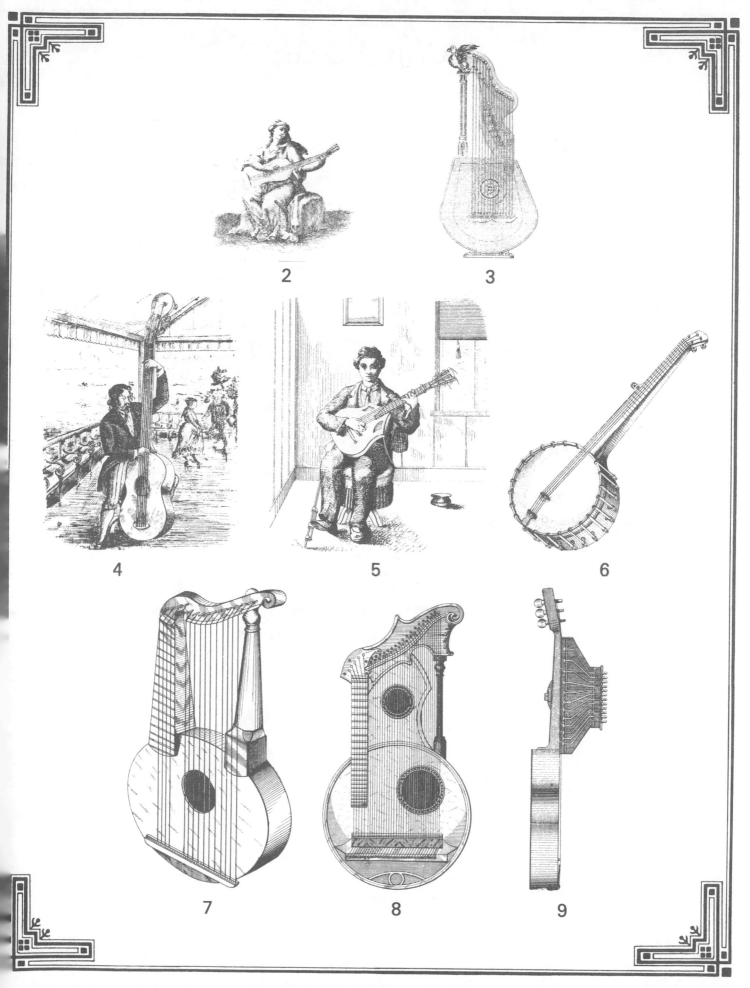

2

3

4

5

6

7

8

9

MUSIC BOXES

THE use of machines for making mechanical music is almost coeval with the invention of clocks.

The principle of their mechanism is almost the same as that of the barrel or hand organ, and of the machinery used for chimes of bells in church towers.

Music boxes proper were not introduced much before the 18th century.

Among the earliest made were small ones, to be worn as charms pendent from a watch chain, and from this insignificant beginning has grown the modern music box, capable of almost every musical effect, and of playing from one to more than one hundred tunes. The principal parts of the mechanism are the comb, the cylinder, and the fly or regulator.

Various attachments or accompaniments, such as bells, drums and castanets, are often applied, and different effects are produced according to the arrangement of the music.

In respect to these effects, music boxes are called mandolines, expressives, quatuors, organocleeds, piccolos, &c. Some have a combination of reeds and pipes, and are called flutes, celestial voices or harmoniphones.

The musical boxes of Prague and Ste. Susanne, in France, are largely exported.

The centers of the manufacture in its present state of mechanical perfection, are Geneva and Ste. Croix, in the Pays de Vaud, Switzerland.

MUSIC BOXES

1. Barrel Organ, 18th Century.
2. Sheet Organ.
3. French Organ—A. D. 1842.
4. English—A. D. 1846.
5. U. S. Patent, Self Acting—A. D. 1849.
6. U. S. Patent, Electro Pneumatic—A. D. 1877.
7. U. S. Patent, Mechanical—A.D. 1879.
8. U. S. Patent, Watch Box—A. D. 1881.
9. U. S. Patent, Mechanical—A. D. 1882.

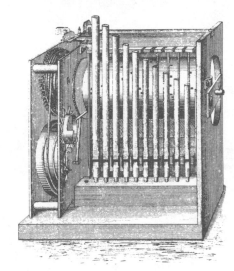

1

2

MUSICAL INSTRUMENTS
429 Manufactories in the United States

	1860	1880
Capital Invested, ..	$4,431,900.00	$14,446,765.00
Value of Productions, ...	6,548,432.00	19,254,739.00
Wages Paid, ...	2,378,520.00	7.098,794.00
Hands Employed,..	4,461	11,350

SUB CLASS
MUSIC BOXES
84 Manufactories of Miscellaneous
Musical Instruments in the United States

Capital Invested,.....................	$654,850.00
Value of Productions,.................	853,746.00
Wages Paid, ...	293,062.00
Hands Employed,....................	573

202 Patents Granted by the United States

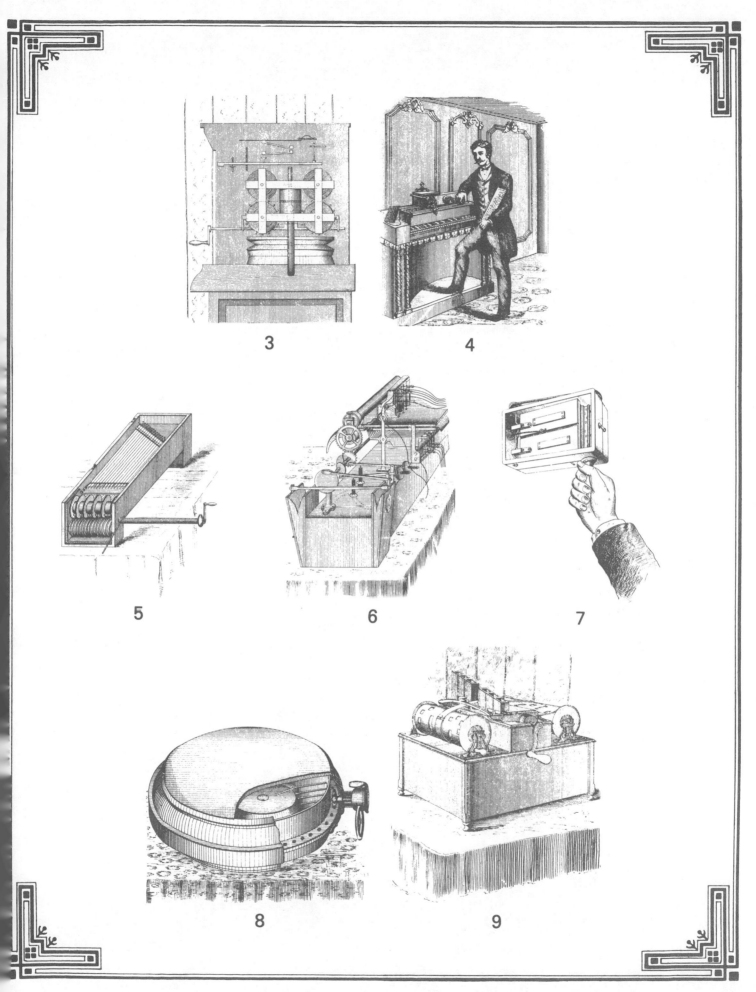

3

4

5

6

7

8

9

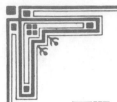

PIANOS

THE first marked approach to the piano-forte appears in the transition from the dulcimer to the keyed cithern, a small, oblong box, holding a series of strings in triangular form, and struck by plectra of quills attached to the inner ends of the keys. This applicaton of the keyboard to stringed instruments is believed to have been first made in the twelfth century.

An improvement on the keyed cithern, called a virginal, was very popular with Queen Elizabeth and the ladies of her time. The first piano was made by Christofali, of Padua, in 1711. In 1716, Marius, a French maker of harpsichords, submitted four forms of instruments "of which he claimed to be the inventor, termed by him hammer harpsichords." Christopher Schroter, in 1717, asserted that he had invented an arrangement of keys, springs and hammers, and stated that "on this instrument he could play at pleasure, forte or piano." This is believed to have suggested the name "piano-forte."

Plenius refers to "forte-pianos" in 1741.

Pedals were introduced about the middle of the eighteenth century, and buff leather was substituted for quills in 1741.

The first piano known in England was made by an English monk, about 1757, at Rome.

The piano was introduced on the stage of Covent Garden Theatre, London, May 16, 1767, as "a new instrument." From this time its success was assured.

Zumpe made large numbers of pianos in England, in 1776.

Bach played upon a "forte-piano" in the palace of Frederick the Great, at Potsdam.

The first upright piano was patented in 1795, by Wm. Stodart.

Few attempts were made at piano making in the United States until the present century.

Jonas Chickering, the founder of the firm of Chickering & Sons, of Boston and New York, has been called the father of the business in this country. He began to manufacture pianos in 1823, and exposed his first instrument for sale on April 15 of that year.

The iron frame and overstrung scale are the two most prominent features in improvements on pianos in America.

Fifteen kinds of wood are used in the ordinary piano.

There were manufactured in the United States, in 1829, 2,500 pianos, of the aggregate value of $75,000. About 15,000 are manufactured yearly in New York alone. The United States now far outstrips Europe in the manufacture of pianos, and possesses the largest establishments in the world.

PIANOS

1. Ancient Lyre.
2. Ancient Harp.
3. Ancient Dulcimer.
4. Ancient Psalterium.
5. Citole, 13th Century.
6. Virginal, 16th Century.
7. English Upright—A. D. 1795.
8. Spinnet—A. D. 1815.
9. Harpsichord—A. D. 1820.
10. U. S. Patent, Square—A. D. 1884.
11. U. S. Patent, Piano Action—A. D. 1884.
12. U. S. Patent, Piano Action—A. D. 1884.

1

MUSICAL INSTRUMENTS
429 Manufactories in the United States

	1860	1880
Capital Invested, ..	$4,431,900.00	$14,446,765.00
Value of Productions, ...	6,548,432.00	19,254,739.00
Wages Paid, ...	2,378,520.00	7,098,794.00
Hands Employed,..	4,461	11,350

SUB CLASS
PIANOS
174 Manufactories in the United States

Capital Invested, ...	$9,869,577.00
Value of Productions, ...	12,264,521.00
Wages Paid, ...	4,663,193.00
Hands Employed, ...	6,575

730 Patents Granted by the United States

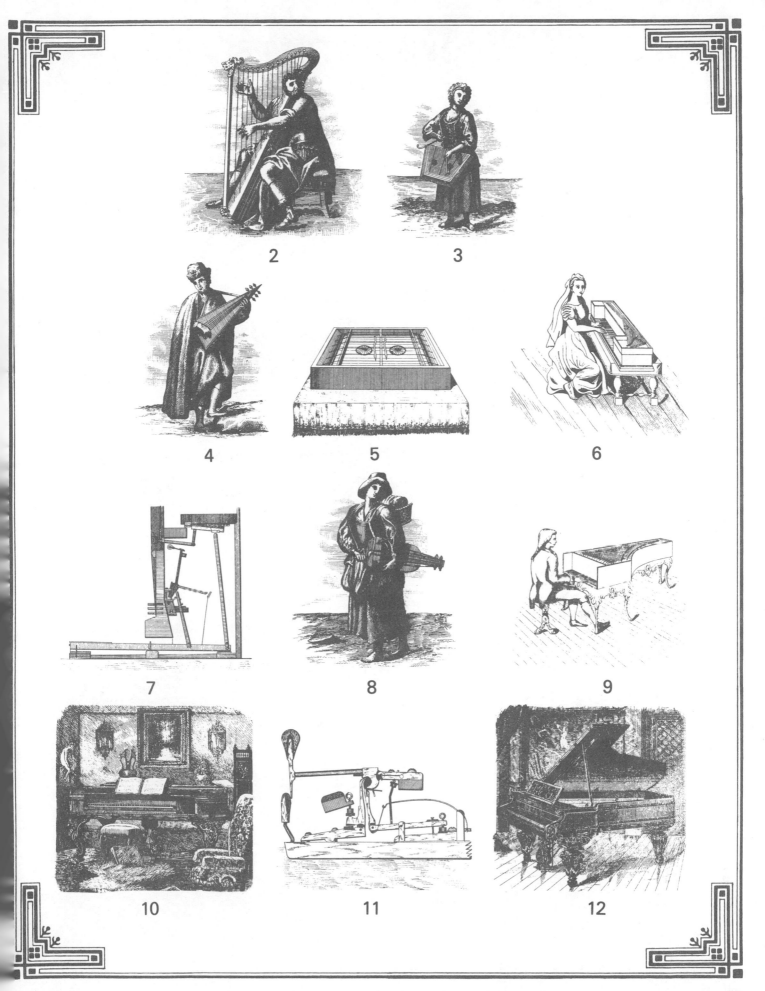

2

3

4

5

6

7

8

9

10

11

12

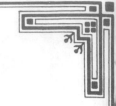

COOKING STOVES

COOKING STOVES

1. Primitive Cooking.
2. U. S. Patent Hot Water Reservoir and Warming Oven—A. D. 1875.
3. U. S. Patent Portable Range—A. D. 1875.
4. U. S. Patent Gasoline Vapor Stove—A. D. 1878.
5. U. S. Patent Oil Stove—A. D. 1878.
6. U. S. Patent Gas Cooking Stove—A. D. 1880.

A PRIMITIVE mode of cooking in use among the savage tribes of New Zealand is called "stone boiling." A hole is dug in the earth, dry wood placed in it, and on that a number of stones; when the stones become red hot the unconsumed fuel is removed, wet green leaves are placed upon the stones, and upon the leaves the food to be cooked, more leaves over the food, and a mat over them all. Water is poured on the mat, and, finally, earth is added as an outside coating; and thus the food is cooked by a combined baking and steaming process.

The North American Indians use stones which have been made red hot in the fire, and put them, one after the other, into a vessel of water containing the food to be cooked.

The Jews were probably the first nation who had any regularly constructed ovens; in which they were followed by the Romans, who erected bake houses for the supply of food for their military.

One of the first attempts at constructing a stove, or closed fire place, was made by Polignac in 1709.

Count Rumford invented a cooking range in 1798; it was lined with brick and soapstone, with ventilating ovens.

The early patterns of cooking stoves were the ten plate oval, with the oven above the fire; the saddle bag pattern came next, the oven being in the middle over the fire; then the horse-block stove, the rear part being a step higher than the front. A rotary was also made, with a movable top to bring any particular vessel directly over the fire. Then came the parent of the modern cook stove, the Buck, for wood and coal, with the fire above the oven, which carried the flame around, behind and below the oven the opening into the stove pipe being about on a level with the oven floor.

COOKING STOVES.

2,446 Patents Granted by the United States.

1

2

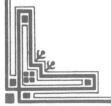

3

4

5

6

CORK EXTRACTORS

THE corkscrew was unknown to our forefathers two hundred years ago.

Various methods of extracting corks were resorted to in olden times, such as winding a cloth or handkerchief tightly around the cork, and with a peculiar jerk pulling the stopper out of the bottle; breaking the neck of the bottle was a common practice, and many persons became very expert in removing corks with the teeth.

The earliest mention of the corkscrew is in an amusing poem entitled "The Tale of the Bottle Screw," in a collection of poems by Nicholas Amhurst, published in 1723. Bacchus is described in the poem, and among other things, it is said of him:

"This hand a corkscrew did contain,
And that a bottle of champagne."

Yet at that time "bottle screw" appears to have been the common name of this useful article, for the poet concludes his tale with the following lines:

"By me shall Birmingham become
In future days more famed than Rome;
Shall owe to me her reputation,
And serve with bottle screws the nation."

The modern corkscrew came into use about the beginning of the last century, and was for many years called a "bottle screw."

Corkscrews, like corks, are to be found, in some shape or other, in all parts of the civilized world.

CORK EXTRACTORS

116 Patents Granted by the United States

CORK EXTRACTORS

1. Primitive Hand.
2. Primitive, Teeth.
3. Primitive, Nail.
4. Primitive, Double Fork.
5. Cork Screw.
6. Cork Screw, Brush Attachment.
7. U. S. Patent, Cork Screw—A. D. 1867.
8. U. S. Patent, Cork Extractor and Cutter—A. D. 1867.
9. U. S. Patent, Cork Extractor—A. D. 1882.

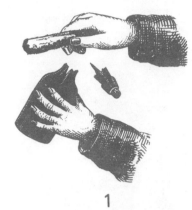

1

2

3

4　　　　5　　　　6

7　　　　8　　　　9

METAL PACKING AND STORING CANS

VASES, made of umbricated or overlapping plates, supposed to be soldered together, are represented on the tombs of Thothmes, 1490 B. C.

The most popular packing and storing cans are the light tin receptacles now manufactured annually by millions. In these are packed fruits and vegetables of all sorts, oils, cocoa, meats, sardines, lobsters, crabs, and in fact everything that is produced on land or sea.

These cans are filled with the desired product, and then rendered air-tight by soldering on a tip top.

Metal packing and storing cans preserve their contents for years in a state of comparative freshness, and have proved a most useful invention.

One of the earliest objections to metal packing cans was the difficulty of opening: to obviate this, a tin pocket on the top was made thinner than the rest of the can, and this pocket ripped open by means of a small wire attached inside, which cut through the thin tin without difficulty.

Shears, or can openers, of peculiar shape, and made for the purpose of cutting through the tin, have also been invented.

When the pork industry became so prominent in the central part of this country, a large tin barrel, with a closely-fitting removable top, was patented, in which lard was packed. Smaller vessels were also used, in which lard was stored for transportation and for daily use.

When the various oils took the place of the tallow and wax candle, the combustible fluid was stored almost entirely in metallic vessels.

An adjustable oil can was constructed, from which the oil could be poured into a smaller can without coming in contact with the air.

Large quantities of food, stored in metallic cans, are consumed in the United States and throughout the entire civilized world. The ships of the Navy and the merchant marine are stored with them.

METAL PACKING AND STORING CANS

2,148 Patents Granted by the United States

Every year the demand increases, and every year invention adds some new device which is calculated to better preserve the contents of the cans.

METAL PACKING AND STORING CANS

1. U. S. Patent, Tilting Carboy—A. D. 1871.
2. U. S. Patent, Rip Patch Can—A. D. 1878.
3. U. S. Patent, Rip Patch Can—A. C. 1878.
4. U. S. Patent, Knock Down Cover Can—A. D. 1879.
5. U.S. Patent, Pyramidal Can—A. D. 1879.
6. U. S. Patent, Double Fish Can—A. D. 1879.
7. U. S. Patent, Fruit Can—A. D. 1879.
8. U. S. Patent, Rip Strip Can—A. D. 1879.
9. U. S. Patent, Rip Side Can—A. D. 1879.
10. U. S. Patent, Shipping and Filling Can—A. D. 1879.
11. U. S. Patent, Safety Shipping Can—A. D. 1881.
12. U. S. Patent, Lamp Filling Can—A. D. 1881.
13. U. S. Patent, Rip Wire Can—A. D. 1881.
14. U.S. Patent, Lamp Filling Can—A. D. 1883.
15. U. S. Patent, Knock Down Cover Can—A. D. 1884.
16. U. S. Patent, Transporting and Dispensing Can—A. D. 1884.

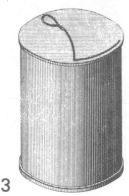

1

2

3

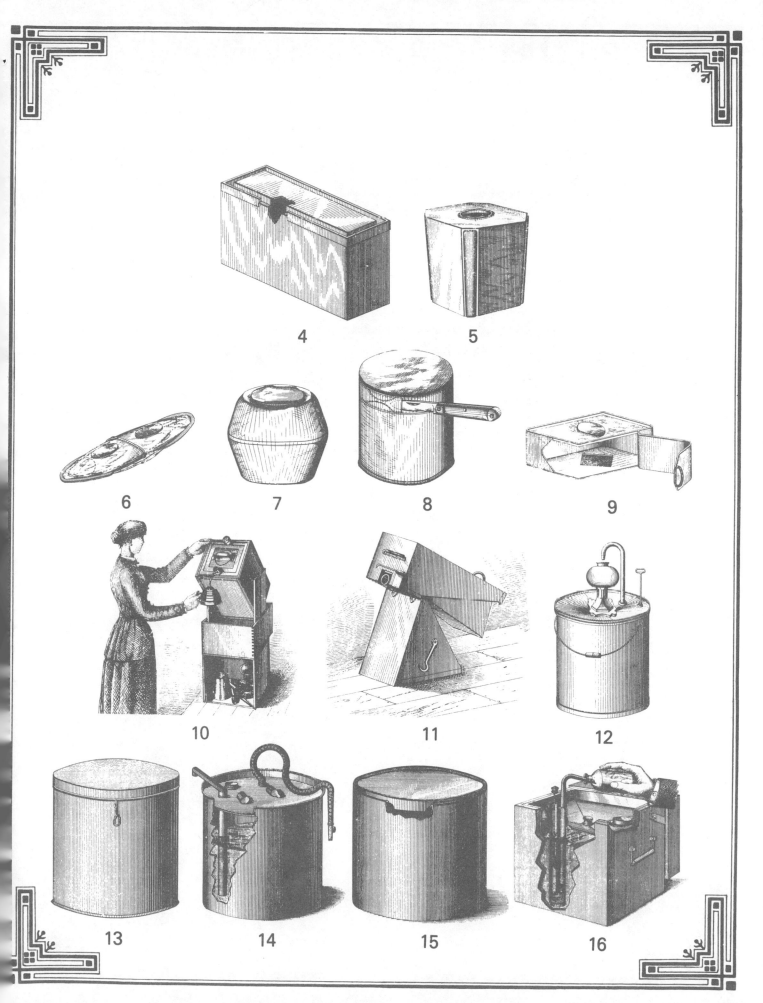

4   5

6   7   8   9

10   11   12

13   14   15   16

PITCHERS, CRUETS AND STAND

PITCHERS are of great antiquity and are frequently referred to in the Bible.

In the last chapter of Ecclesiastes we read:

"Or ever the silver cord be loosed, or the golden bowl be broken, or the pitcher be broken at the fountain, or the wheel broken at the cistern."

These beautiful figures of speech indicate the remoteness of the history of the vessels therein referred to.

The modern tea pot, oil jars, the common pitcher, vases, &c., are all to be seen in Egyptian paintings.

The most primitive way of carrying water and wine was in carefully tanned skins. This was followed by a crude style of pottery, remains of which are to be found in almost every quarter of the globe.

The Romans used many styles of pitchers.

Modern invention has produced most beautiful shapes and designs. These are made of china, porcelain, alabaster, silver, and the most costly of gold.

Pitchers are of every conceivable shape and variety, and yet each different design is readily recognized.

Molasses pitchers are of glass or china, with a silver lid. A wine pitcher is of cut glass with a stopper something like that of a decanter.

A most useful invention is the silver ice pitcher. These show great varieties. The first patent was a plain pitcher with a closely-fitting lid. Later inventors devised the tilting ice pitcher, with a spout something like an ordinary spigot. This patent has been very generally utilized. Silver stands for coffee, tea, &c., are now made with this spout, so as to tilt at the slightest motion of the hand.

The revolving cruet is common to every household. The glass bottles that fit into the silver holes are for various condiments used for seasoning food. This is an ancient vessel. The epicures of

Rome used them made of precious metals.

Modern casters are of many different shapes and sizes; the commonest has a silver case, in which fits six bottles; a smaller caster has only two or three bottles. A useful and portable caster is made of twisted silver wire, with only three small bottles.

Pickle stands, celery stands and other similar appliances of the table may be properly mentioned under this head.

PITCHERS, CRUETS AND STANDS

1. U. S. Patent, Molasses Pitcher—A. D. 1855.
2. U. S. Patent, Molasses Pitcher—A. D. 1857.
3. U. S. Patent, Pitcher Lid—A. D. 1860.
4. U. S. Patent, Pitcher—A. D. 1866.
5. U. S. Patent, Sirup Pitcher—A. D. 1869.
6. U. S. Patent, Ice Pitcher—A. D. 1871.
7. U. S. Patent, Molasses Jug—A. D. 1872.
8. U. S. Patent, Tilting Cruet—A. D. 1877.
9. U. S. Patent, Ice Pitcher Stand—A. D. 1879.
10. U. S. Patent, Tilting Pitcher—A. D. 1881.
11. U. S. Patent, Detachable Pitcher Spout—A. D. 1882.
12. U. S. Patent, Tilting Vessel—A. D. 1884.

1

TABLE ARTICLES

PITCHERS, CRUETS AND STANDS

271 Patents Granted by the United States

2

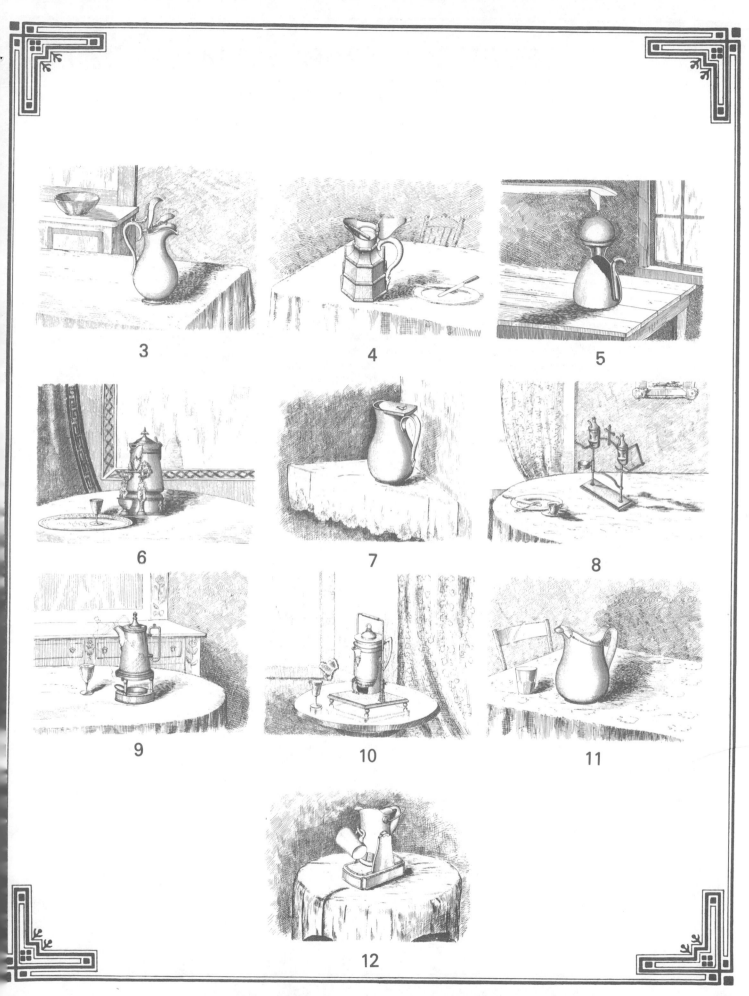

3

4

5

6

7

8

9

10

11

12

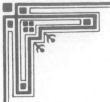
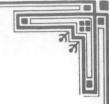

SEWING MACHINES AND ATTACHMENTS

THE first attempts of a mechanical contrivance for reducing the labor of sewing, as was natural, were rather close imitations of hand sewing, though they introduced features essential to the most improved sewing machines. The ancient tambourine apparatus for embroidering figures upon fabrics, to be afterwards removed and sewed upon others, combined the eye pointed needle with other devices now common in sewing machines.

The earliest patent on sewing machines appears to have been granted in England to C. F. Weisenthal, June 24, 1755. His patent was for the needle with the eye in the center and pointed at both ends. The device was operated by hand.

Saint's machine (English patent of July, 1790,) is the nearest approach to the modern apparatus, but was adapted only to leather sewing, as the notched needle which pushed the thread through could not have been used for fibrous material.

In 1825, Thimmonnier, a poor tailer of France, conceived the idea of a sewing apparatus, and for sixteen years labored to develop it. In 1834 he obtained a patent for a crocheting machine adapted to sewing purposes. He achieved substantial success and in 1841 two hundred of his machines were at work making army clothing.

A machine was patented February 21, 1842, in the United States, by J. J. Greenough, for making the through and through stitch, having a double pointed needle with an eye in the middle, which was drawn through the cloth by pincers.

Benjamin W. Bean in 1843, patented a machine for making a running or basting stitch, the needle passing through the corrugations of the cloth.

In 1845, Elias Howe, of Cambridge, Mass., completed his first machine and obtained a patent thereon Setember 10, 1846. This was the first complete sewing machine designed for general purposes.

His principle covered the forming of the seam "by carrying a thread through the cloth by means of a curved needle on the end of a vibrating arm, and the passing of a shuttle furnished with its bobbin between the needle and the thread which it carried."

Mr. Howe, almost immediately after obtaining his patent, went to Europe to obtain capital for the manufacture of his machine, but he was met by a scepticism even more obdurate and discouraging than he encountered from those to whom he applied for aid in the United States. He returned home after two years, in a sailing vessel, paying for his passage by manual labor, and arriving literally penniless.

Singer's first patent was granted in 1851.

The first rotating hook was patented by Wilson in 1851.

Gibbs invented the rotating hook which produced a twist in the looping stitch.

Wilcox invented the automatic tension.

The Grover & Baker machine of 1852 first introduced the double loop stitch employing two threads effected by a circular horizontally moving needle.

The vibratory eye-pointed needle, the reciprocating shuttle, the rotating hook and the four-motion feed, are the essential foundation elements of sewing machines.

Sewing machine attachments are classified as follows: Binders, holders, bobbin winders, braiders, corders, guides, hemmers, needle clamps, presser feed and lifters, rufflers and gatherers, setters and threaders, take ups, tensions, needles, shuttles, bobbins, thread cutters, trimmers, tuck creasers, markers, tucking guides, &c.

SEWING MACHINES AND ATTACH—MENTS.

1. Primitive Hand Sewing.
2. English Chain Stitch—A. D. 1790.
3. U. S. Patent, Lock Stitch—A. D. 1846.
4. U. S. Patent, Lock Stitch—A. D. 1851.
5. U. S. Patent, Four Motion Feed—A. D. 1852.
6. U. S. Patent, Chain Stitch—A. D. 1857.
7. U. S. Patent, Button Hole—A. D. 1881.
8. U. S. Patent, Button Hole—A. D. 1881.
9. Machine Sewing—A. D. 1884.
10. Gatherer or Ruffler—A. D. 1884.
11. Plate Hemmer and Binder—A. D. 1884.
12. Feller—A. D. 1884.
13. Quilter—A. D. 1884.
14. Corder—A. D. 1884.
15. Braider—A.D. 1884.

SEWING MACHINES AND ATTACHMENTS.

106 Manufactories in the United States

	1860	1880
Capital Invested ..	$1,427,750.00	$12,501,830.00
Value of Productions,....	4,255,820.00	13,863,188.00
Wages Paid,.....	1,094,796.00	4,636,099.00
Hands Employed,	2,297	9,553

3,841 Patents Granted by the United States

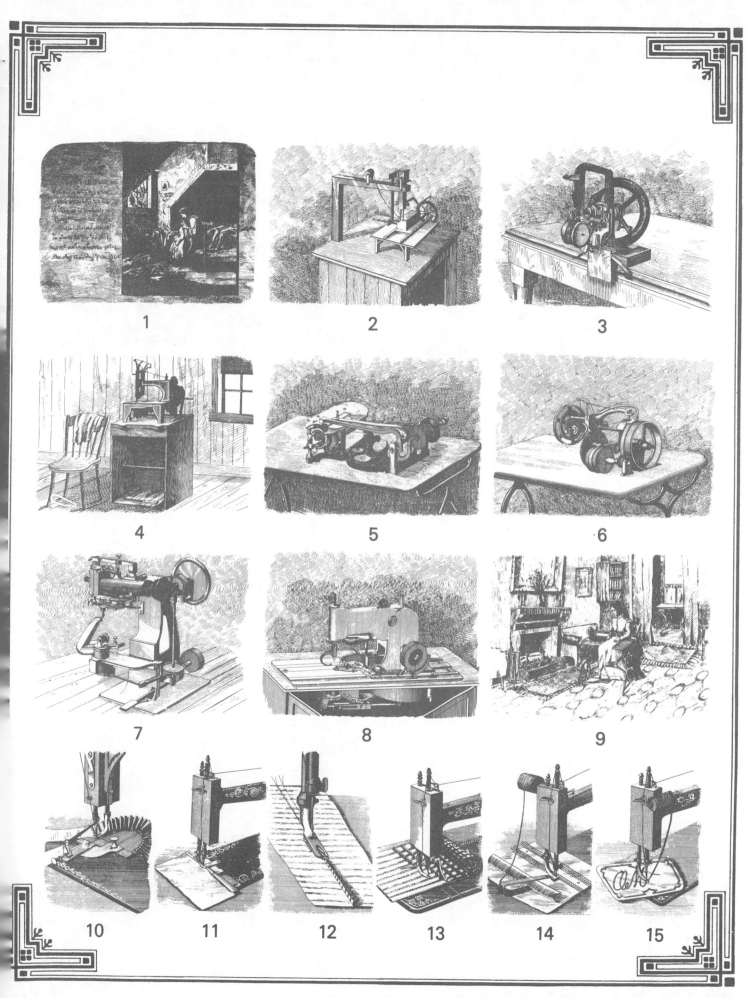

1

2

3

4

5

6

7

8

9

10

11

12

13

14

15

WASHING MACHINES

CLOTHES were formerly washed by rubbing or stamping upon them in water, or beating them against rough bodies.

The following modes of washing by machinery are embraced in the modern machine:

1st, Churning; the clothes are beaten by a pounder in a tub. 2nd, the Dash Wheel. 3d, Sluicing, the hot water being driven through the clothes. 4th, Centrifugal. 5th, Twisting. 6th, Squeezing. 7th, Rolling. 8th, Rubbing. 9th, Rocking.

Millions of washboards are made and sold in the United States every year, and at least 7,200,000 are sold yearly.

There are two factories in Cleveland which turn out 200 dozen washboards a day, and one in Toledo which turns out over a million a year.

There are at least twenty different varieties of washboards, and the best are made in the West.

The Eastern factories make their washboards of pine.

The best wood for washboards is cotton wood or sycamore; pine is too soft, and white pine is too expensive. The best are made with dovetailed heads, with wire nails driven across the grain of the wood.

1

2

WASHING MACHINES
61 Manufactories in the United States

	1860	1880
Capital Invested, ..	$34,700.00	$652,549.00
Value of Productions, ...	87,565.00	1,182,714.00
Wages Paid, ...	29,124.00	176,287.00
Hands Employed,..	85	476

	Primitive Mode	Present Machine
CAPACITY—		
Shirts per day, ...	50	600
Hands Employed per day, ...	1	1

2,458 Patents Granted by the United States

WASHING MACHINES

1. Primitive Indian Dhobees.
2. Colonial.
3. Hand.
4. U. S. Patent, Vertical Rubber—A. D. 1869.
5. U. S. Patent, Boiler—A. D. 1874.
6. U. S. Patent, Vertical Pounder—A. D. 1878.
7. U. S. Patent, Rotary Steam—A. D. 1880.
8. U. S. Patent, Oscillating Rubber—A. D. 1882.
9. U. S. Patent, Rotary Rubber—A. D. 1883.
10. U. S. Patent, Vertical Rubber—A. D. 1883.
11. U. S. Patent, Inclined Rubber—A. D. 1883.
12. U. S. Patent, Vertical Pounder—A. D. 1884.

3

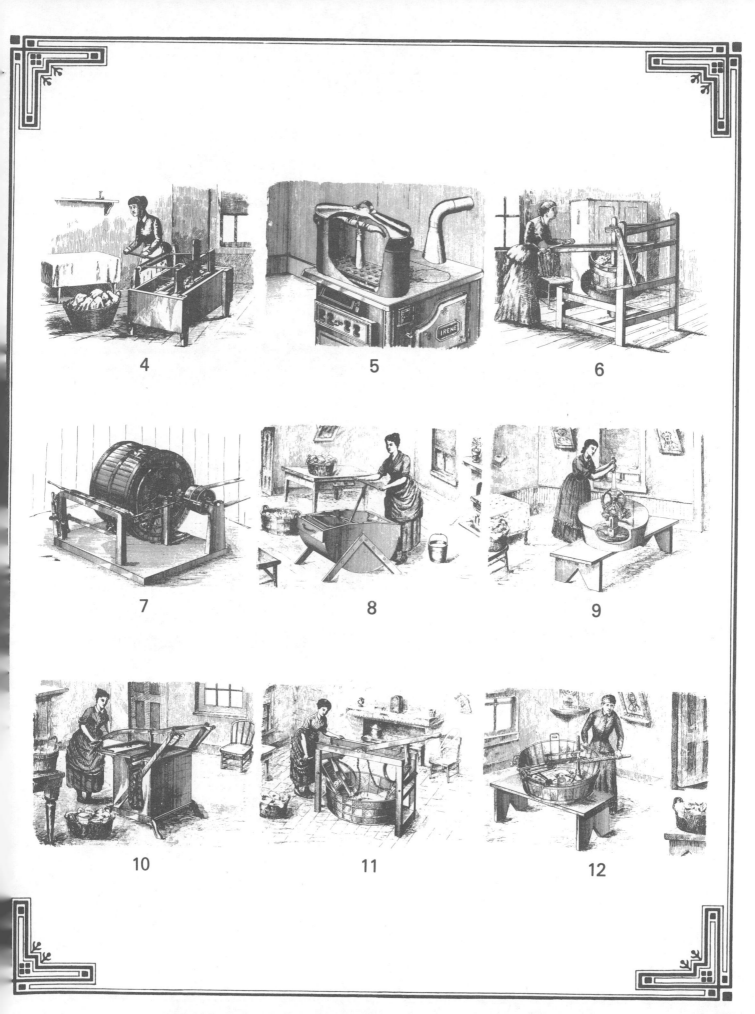

4

5

6

7

8

9

10

11

12

WRINGERS

THE ordinary clothes wringer used by the washerwoman is a wooden frame with rollers, through which the wet articles are passed to squeeze out the water. These rollers are governed by a common wooden screw, which forces them closer together or allows them to separate as heavier or lighter fabrics are to be passed through them.

But the laundry requires a better machine, and those most in use are the "Tolhurst Extractor," the "Universal," and the "Novelty" wringers.

The first of these consists of a perforated copper basket, enclosed in a clyindrical case. This basket is made to revolve at the rate of a thousand revolutions to the minute, which drives out all the water.

The "Universal" and "Novelty" wringers consist of two parallel rolls of vulcanized rubber, fitted to double-geared shafts. The uppermost roll is set in loose boxes, and pressure is applied by means of a wooden spring. To prevent the rolls from softening by use, they are treated to several coats of varnish, then wound with linen thread, and varnish applied to this, after which they are covered with rubber cement.

1

2

3

WRINGERS

61 Manufactories of Washing Machines and Wringers in the United States

	1860	1880
Capital Invested, ..	$34,700.00	$652,549.00
Value of Productions, ...	87,565.00	1,182,714.00
Wages Paid, ...	29,124,00	176,287.00
Hands Employed,..	85	476

	Primitive Mode	Present Machine
CAPACITY—		
Shirts per day, ...	50	600
Hands Employed per day, ...	1	1

510 Patents Granted by the United States

WRINGERS

1. Hand.
2. U. S. Patent, Machine—A. D. 1847.
3. U. S. Patent, Adjustable Roll—A. D. 1855.
4. U. S. Patent, Adjustable Roll—A.D. 1861.
5. U. S. Patent, Roller—A. D. 1862.
6. U. S. Patent, Roller—A. D. 1872.
7. U. S. Patent, Roller—A. D. 1872.
8. U. S. Patent, Roller—A. D. 1875.
9. U. S. Patent, Roller—A. D. 1878.

4

5

6

7

8

9

A WOODEN tool of the same shape as the common flat iron has been discovered in Thebes. It was used for smoothing and pressing cloth, and is about six inches in length, and made of very hard wood.

The ordinary flat iron, heated before a fire, or on a stove, with which the laundry maid, by muscular force, ironed out clothing, has become almost a thing of the past. Even where the iron is now used, it is generally heated either by a flexible tube from the gas jet, or by a fire inside of the iron itself. Even the mangle has given place to improved ironing machines, some heated by steam, which iron with equal facility the most delicate piece of lace or the coarsest fabric worn, whilst the fluting attachment does away with the fluting scissors and the deft fingers which used them.

In the latest improved devices, the article which requires washing, no matter how elaborate its make-up, is simply passed through a series of machines and comes out washed, starched, fluted, ironed and polished.

The first steam laundry in the United States was started in Boston, Massachusetts, in 1853. Several, located in New York city, employ from 100 to 150 hands each.

The Empire laundry turns out more than 100,000 pieces per month. It is said that from ten to twenty thousand persons are employed in New York city alone in laundry work.

1

IRONING

	Primitive Mode	Present Machine
CAPACITY— Doz. Cuffs or Collars per day, ...	50	600
Hands Employed per day, ...	2	2

551 Patents Granted by the United States

2

IRONING

1. Flat Iron.
2. U. S. Patent, Sad Iron—A.D. 1852.
3. U. S. Patent, Smoothing Iron—A. D. 1873.
4. U. S. Patent, Ironing Machine—A. D. 1878.
5. U. S. Patent, Ironing Machine—A. D. 1879.
6. U. S. Patent, Ironing Machine—A. D. 1882.
7. U. S. Patent, Cuff and Collar Ironer—A. D. 1882.
8. U. S. Patent, Smoothing and Fluting Iron—A. D. 1882.
9. U. S. Patent, Ironing Machine—A. D. 1884.

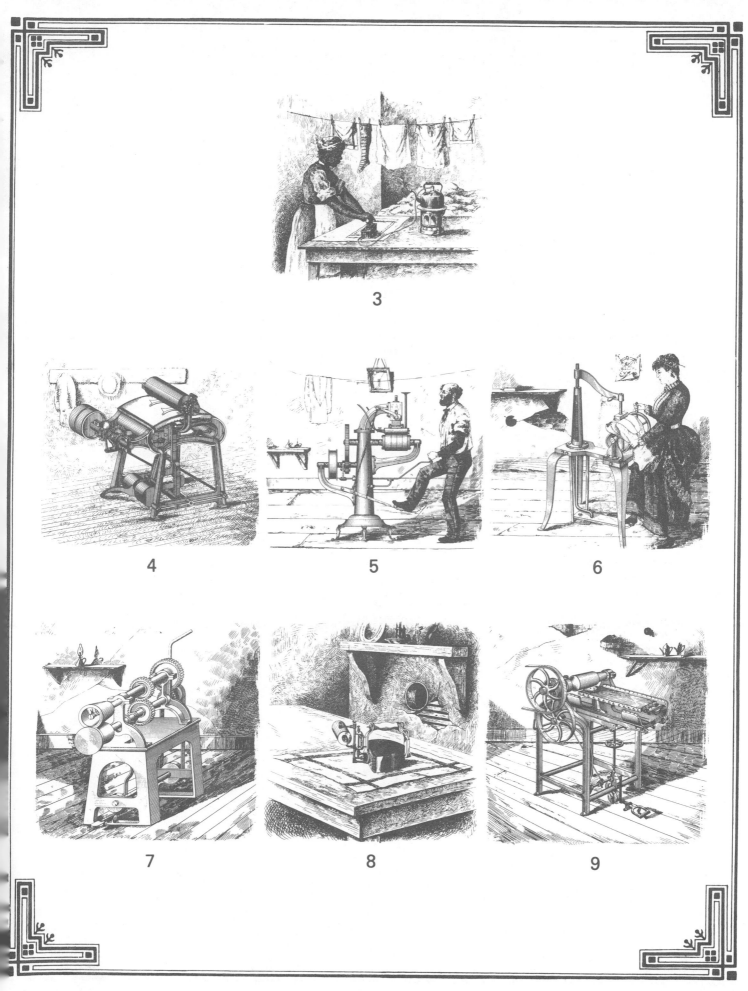

3

4

5

6

7

8

9

BOOTS AND SHOES

HOMER speaks of the "brazen-booted" Greeks.

Moses said of Asher: "Thy shoes shall be iron and brass."

The Egyptians and Hebrews had some protection for their feet at the time of Abraham, for the patriarch refused to "take even as much as a shoe latchet from the King of Sodom, lest he should say he had made him (Abraham) rich."

The Chinese have made shoes, from time immemorial, from skin, silk, rushes, linen, wool, wood and metal.

Succeeding ages introduced foot coverings of various kinds; the sandal, the moccasin, slippers, buskins, &c.

Syrian boots were of leather, and had an extra thickness sewed below to answer for a sole.

Hesiod, 1,000 B. C., mentions "oxhide boots as part of the winter equipments of a plowman."

Among the trades practiced by the Egyptians was shoemaking. An illustration on the tombs at Thebes is shown of a shoemaker at his bench engaged in boring holes with an awl in a leather sole.

The Egyptians made shoes of leather, papyrus and textile fabrics. The upper was sewed to the sole without a heel.

Pliny said "Tychius invented the leather shoe." The "Caliga" of the Romans was the coarse shoe of the soldier, the sole being thickly studded with nails.

The Roman Emperors wore shoes enriched with jewels and embroidered with gold and silver. The shoes of the Emperor Marcus Aurelius had separate apartments for the toes.

The shoes of the Roman senators reached to the middle of the leg.

Julius Caesar wore high heeled shoes to increase his stature.

In England, shoes of a similar form to those of the present time were worn by the lower classes as early as the 8th century.

From the 12th to the 15th century fashionable shoes in England were made with long toes stuffed with tow; these toes or beaks were so long that it was common to fasten them to the knees of the wearer by a silver chain; in 1463 Parliament limited the length of this useless projection to two inches.

In the American Colonies few, if any, shoes were made from calf skin. Cow hide was used almost exclusively for foot gear.

As early as 1635 the town of Lynn, Mass., had a shoemaker. In 1877 the product of the Lynn factories was not less than 14,000,000 pairs of boots and shoes.

A single shoe factory in Massachusetts turns out as many pairs of boots as 30,000 boot makers in Paris, France.

The manufacture of boots and shoes in the United States in 1880 is reported as producing to the value of $166,050,354; the materials consumed included 6,831,661 sides of sole leather, 21,147,656 sides of upper leather, and 32,960,614 pounds of other leather; the products were 30,690,896 pairs of boots and 98,887,615 pairs of shoes.

BOOTS AND SHOES

1. Egyptian Sandal of Palm—1495 B. C.
2. Assyrian Sandal—669 B. C.
3. Persian Boot—500 B.C.
4. Roman Cothurmus—A. D. 275.
5. Anglo-Saxon Bandaged Leather Hose—8th Century.
6. French Boot—17th Century.
7. U. S. Patent, Pegged Shoe—A. D. 1811.
8. U. S. Patent, Rubber Shoe—A.D. 1834.
9. U. S. Patent, Congress Gaiter—A.D. 1840.
10. U. S. Patent, Machine Sewed—A. D. 1860.
11. U. S. Patent, Cable Screw Wire—A. D. 1867.
12. Modern Boot and Shoe.

BOOTS AND SHOES

18,389 Manufactories in the United States

	1860	1880
Capital Invested, ..	$23,357,627.00	$58,973,665.00
Value of Productions, ...	91,889,298.00	217,093,627.00
Wages Paid, ...	30,938,080.00	53,820,864.00
Hands Employed,..	123,026	143,201

1,974 Patents Granted by the United States

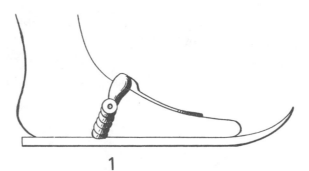

1

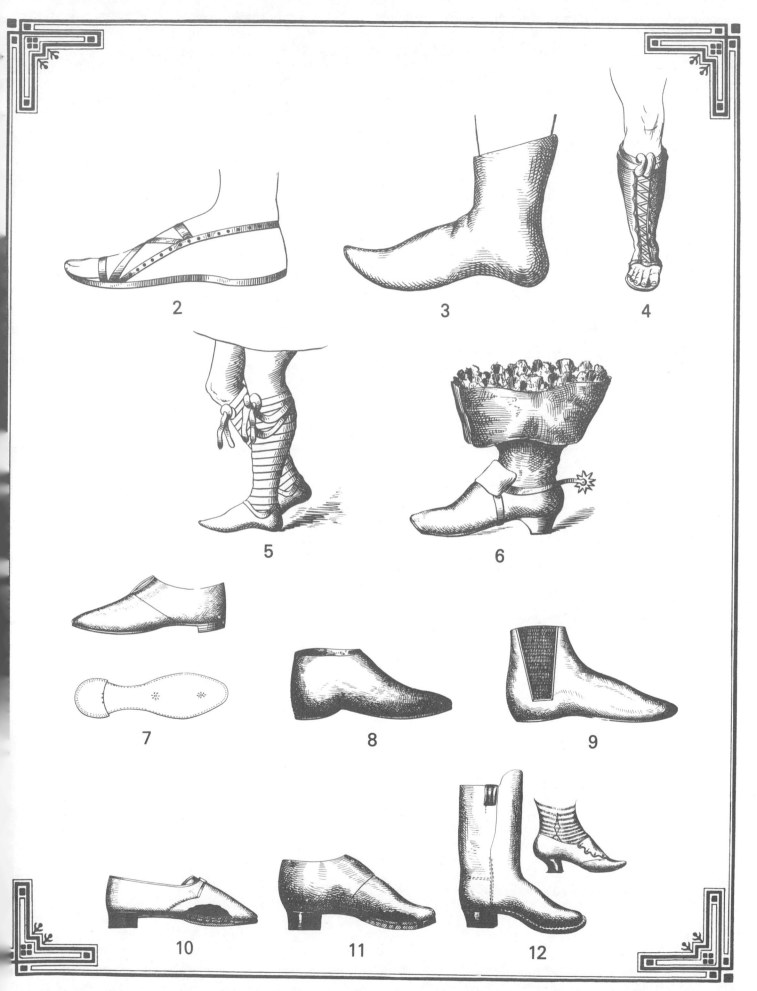

2

3

4

5

6

7

8

9

10

11

12

FIRE ARMS

THE invention of Portable Fire Arms is attributed to the Italians, and the year 1430 has been named as the time of their introduction. The earliest record of their introduction into England is in 1471, when Edward IV landed at Ravenspur with 900 Flemings, armed with hand guns.

The Dutch invented the apparatus for striking fire by the friction of a small steel wheel against a piece of iron pyrites. This was known as the wheel lock.

The flint lock was introduced during the reign of Queen Elizabeth, about 1692, and was superseded by the percussion lock in 1807.

An interesting model, showing the revolving cylinder of a fire arm (upon which the Colt's principle of the Colt revolver is based.) is to be seen in the Museum at the Washington Navy Yard, such model having been presented by the British Government, and is said to have been made during the reign of Queen Elizabeth.

Henry VIII, of England, took great interest in fire arms, and two weapons made during his reign are still in existence, and are said to resemble the modern Snider rifle.

Among the curiosities of this branch of invention is Pickles' English Patent of 1718, wherein is described the use of "round bullets for Christians and square ones for Turks."

The first U. S. patent granted for a breech loader was to Thornton and Hall, May 21st, 1811. Between that time and 1839 over 10,000 of these arms were made and issued to the troops in garrison on the frontier.

Prior to the war of 1861-65 the principal breech loaders were known as Sharps, Burnside, Maynards, Merrills and Spencers.

The Martini gun was invented by a Swiss.

The Chassepot is a French invention.

The United States has adopted the Springfield pattern of gun, manufactured at the Springfield Arsenal, Mass., after the systems of Allen and of Stillman; England the Snider improved; France the Chassepot; Belgium the Albini; Holland the Snyder; Austria the Wanzel; Turkey the Remington and Winchester; Sweden the Hagstorm; Russia the Laidley and Berdan; Switzerland the Winchester; Portugal the Westley-Richards; Prussia the Needle Gun.

Breech loaders purchased by the United States between 1861 and 1866 were of the following kinds and numbers of each; Spencer, 94,136; Sharps, 80,512; Burnside, 55,567; Smith, 30,062; Starr, 25,603; Gallaher, 22,728; Maynard, 20,002; Remington, 20,000; Merrill, 14,495; Joslyn, 11,261; Cosmopolitan, 9,342; Warner, 4,001; Hall, 3,520; Gibbs, 1,052; Ballard, 1,500; Ball, 1,002; Palmer, 1,001; Snyder, 892; Wesson, 151.

FIRE ARMS

1. German Flint Lock Pistol, 16th Century.
2. Match Lock, 16th Century.
3. Muzzle Loader, 19th Century.
4. U. S. Patent, Revolver—A. D. 1850.
5. U. S. Patent, Magazine Gun—A. D. 1865.
6. U. S. Patent, Breech Loader—A. D. 1875.
7. U. S. Patent, Revolver—A. D. 1882.
8. U. S. Patent, Electric Gun—A. D. 1883.
9. U. S. Patent, Breech Loader—A. D. 1884.

FIRE ARMS

39 Manufactories in the United States

	1860	1880
Capital Invested, ..	$466,000.00	8,115,489.00
Value of Productions, ...	891,344.00	5,736,936.00
Wages Paid	95,016.00	2,700,281.00
Hands Employed,..	308	4,672

2,446 Patents Granted in the United States

1

2

3

4

5

6

7

8

9

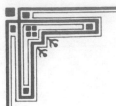

CARTRIDGES

CARTRIDGES are of modern invention. The original custom was to use loose powder and ball. Gustavus Adolphus in 1632 made up the first cartridge with a measured quantity of powder and ball attached. Sir James Turner, in the time of Charles II of England, speaks of cartridges used by horsemen carried in a patron. Subsequently cartridges were carried in cases suspended from bandoliers. Still later the cartridge box was adopted, and in modified form is still in use.

Round ball and buck, and ball cartridge are now out of use. They were made of a paper cylinder, which was partially filled with powder and choked near its mid-length by twine, the powder occupying one end and the ball the other; Colt covered his cartridges with tinfoil, and afterwards with paper saturated with nitrate of potassa. The American process of drawing out the blanks for metallic cartridge cases into tubes has been adopted in the European service. The use of metal for this purpose originated with the French. In 1826 Cazalt patented a cartridge of this kind; one of the earliest cartridges was patented by Roberts, of Paris, in 1834. Smith & Wesson took out patents in 1854 and 1860. The fulminate in the first of these was contained in a capsule at the base, in the latter in an annulus within the flange surrounding the base of the cartridge, secured in place by a pasteboard disk.

The metallic cartridge is generally in use throughout the United States and Europe.

CARTRIDGES

311 Patents Granted by the United States

CARTRIDGES

1. U. S. Patent, Paper—A. D. 1858.
2. U. S. Patent, Gut—A. D. 1862.
3. U. S. Patent, Outer Paper Case—A. D. 1862.
4. U. S. Patent, Fibrous Stopper—A. D. 1863.
5. U. S. Patent, Charged—A. D. 1863.
6. U. S. Patent, Interior Fire—A. D. 1866.
7. U. S. Patent, Paper Reinforced—A. D. 1869.
8. U. S. Patent, Electric—A. D. 1883.
9. U. S. Patent, Paper Shell and Metal Base—A.D. 1884.

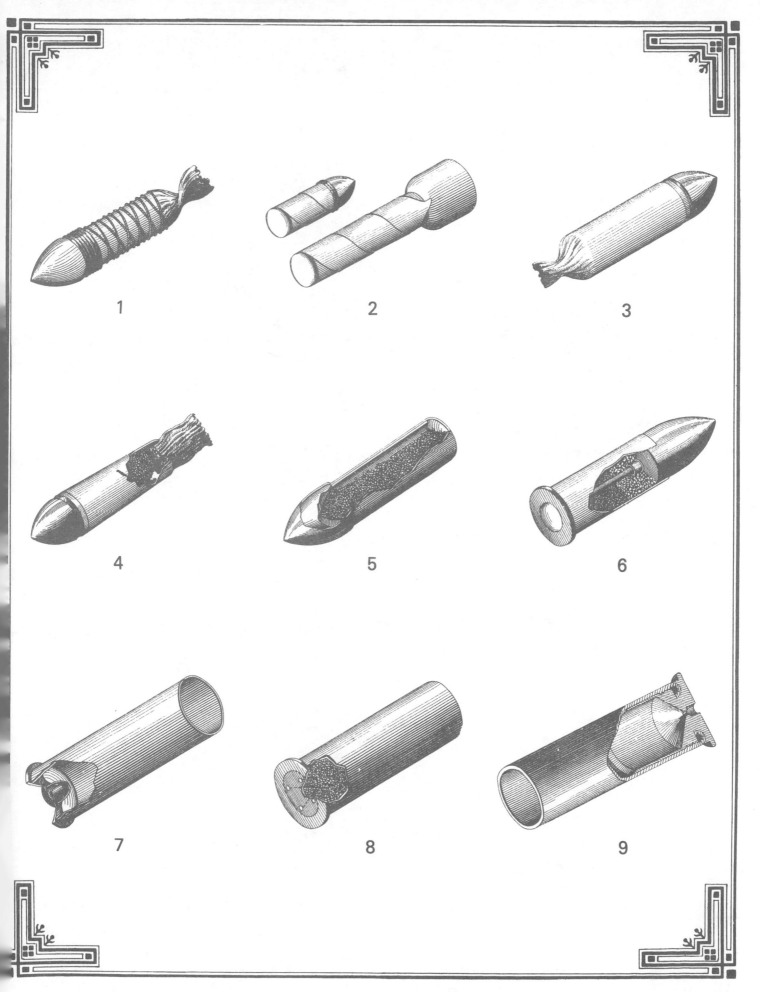

1

2

3

4

5

6

7

8

9

VELOCIPEDES

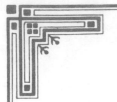

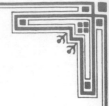

IN the early part of the year 1816 a very curious machine was constructed and used near Rochelle, France. It consisted of two wheels of equal size, placed one in front of the other, connected by a bar on which was a small seat. It was operated by the rider striking his feet against the ground.

This appears to have the progenitor of the bicycle.

In the early part of the present century a machine called the celeripede was invented. The English "Dandy Horse" came into use about sixty years ago.

The first application of the wrench axle was patented in the United States, by P. W. Mackenzie, in 1862.

In the years 1868 and 1869 the velocipede came into sudden popularity, but was superseded by the bicycle, which was imported from England.

The first approved bicycle was exhibited at the Centennial Exhibition, in 1876.

The first American company for the manufacture of bicycles was organized in 1878.

It is estimated that 6,000 were manufactured and sold in the United States in 1884, and that 30,000 were in use in the United States in 1885.

1

VELOCIPEDES

	1878	1884
Number Manufactories,...	1	8
Number in use in the United States,	25	30,000
Number Manufactured, ...	150	9,000

700 Patents Granted by the United States

2

VELOCIPEDES

1. Hand Propeller—A. D. 1700.
2. French Pedal—A. D. 1750.
3. French Hand Propeller—A. D. 1770.
4. American Hand Propeller—A. D. 1804.
5. English Dandy Horse—A. D. 1818.
6. U. S. Patent, Tricycle—A. D. 1864.
7. U. S. Patent, Tricycle—A. D. 1865.
8. U. S. Patent, Bicycle—A. D. 1866.
9. U. S. Patent, Unicycle—A. D. 1869.
10. U. S. Patent, Bicycle—A. D. 1880.
11. U. S. Patent, Tandem—A. D. 1882.
12. U. S. Patent, Ice—A. D. 1883.
13. U. S. Patent, Tricycle—A. D. 1883.
14. U. S. Patent, Bicycle—A. D. 1884.
15. U. S. Patent, Bicycle—A. D. 1884.
16. U. S. Patent, Sociable—A. D. 1884.

3

4

5

6

7

8

9

10

11

12

13

14

15

16

CARRIAGES

THE vehicle used by Joseph to carry his father to Canaan was an ox-cart.

In ancient times horses were only used to draw chariots.

The vehicles of Egypt were two-wheeled, and were known 2000 B. C.

The natives of China and India used carts from an early date.

The Orcera was a carriage used by sick and infirm persons.

A later invention was the Carpenturin; it is represented on antique coins as a two-wheeled car with an arched covering.

The Scythians covered their wagons with felt and leather.

The use of pleasure carriages in Rome was forbidden during the Republic.

The Romans had vehicles with one wheel, adapted to be drawn by horses.

Carriages, the bodies of which were suspended by means of leather straps, were brought into use during the reign of Louis XIV, in the year 1643.

In the sixteenth century carriages were introduced into Spain, Portugal and other countries.

Stage wagons were introduced into France in 1654.

The first carriage built in the United States is said to have been made in 1805, at Dorchester, Mass.

The woods usually used in the manufacture of carriages are hickory, black walnut, cherry, maple, yellow poplar, locust and gum.

1

2

CARRIAGES

3,841 Manufactories in the United States

	1860	1880
Capital Invested, ..	$14,131,537.00	$37,973,493.00
Value of Productions, ...	26,848,905.00	64,951,617.00
Wages Paid, ...	10,001,891.00	18,988,615.00
Hands Employed,..	27,461	45,394

11,013 Patents Granted by the United States

CARRIAGES

1. U. S. Patent, Elliptic Spring Road Buggy—A. D. 1826.
2. U. S. Patent, Jump Seat Carriage—A. D. 1858.
3. U. S. Patent, Rockaway—A.D. 1858.
4. U. S. Patent, Buck Board—A. D. 1876.
5. U. S. Patent, Trotting Sulky—A. D. 1880.
6. U. S. Patent, Buck Board Farm Wagon—A. D. 1883.
7. U. S. Patent, Road Cart—A. D. 1883.
8. U. S. Patent, Side Bar Buggy—A. D. 1884.
9. U. S. Patent, Side Spring Phaeton—A. D. 1884.

3

4

5

6

7

8

9

COACHES

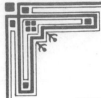

COVERED coaches were known in the fifteenth century, and were used only by women of the first rank, as men thought it disgraceful to ride in them.

Walter Rippin made the first coaches in England in 1555. They were heavy, without springs, and the driver rode on one of the horses.

Coaches to be let for hire were first established in London in 1625.

Glass windows were added to coaches in 1631.

In Amsterdam coaches with wheels were forbidden in 1663, in order to save the pavements of the streets; the bodies were placed on runners.

The Hungarians claim the invention of the modern coach, and say it derived its name from Kotsee, and their king, Cervius, was the first who rode in one.

Coaches were first used in Boston, Mass., in 1669.

Stage coaches were introduced into England by Jethro Tull in 1750, and first employed to carry the mails in 1784. There were six carriage shops in New York City in 1788.

Hackney coaches, drawn by two horses, have generally given place in London to the one-horse cabs, which came into use in 1823.

The long coach, or omnibus, first appeared in Paris in 1827, and in 1830 it was first run on Broadway, New York City.

The English stage coach carries six inside and fourteen outside, in addition to the driver and guard.

Stage and mail coaches are of similar construction, and are used for the same purpose in the United States. They may be drawn by two, four or six horses.

The modern Amercan mail coaches, running at the rate of ten miles an hour over the best turnpike roads, changing horses at every stage, were the finest in the world, but they have been superseded by the net-work of railroads which now cover the country.

COACHES

1. English, Queen Elizabeth.
2. English, Charles II.
3. English, Landeau—A. D. 1757.
4. English, Britzska.
5. English, Post Chaise.
6. Elliptic Spring—A. D. 1805.
7. U. S. Patent, Stage Coach—A. D. 1830.
8. U. S. Patent, Clarence—A. D. 1880.
9. U. S. Patent, Caleche—A. D. 1883.

1

2

COACHES

3,841 Manufactories of Carriages and Wagons in the United States.

	1860	1880
Capital Invested, ..	$14,131,537.00	$37,973,493.00
Value of Productions.....	26,848,905.00	64,951,617.00
Wages Paid, ...	10,001,891.00	18,988,615.00
Hands Employed ..	27,461	45,394

174 Patents Granted by the United States.

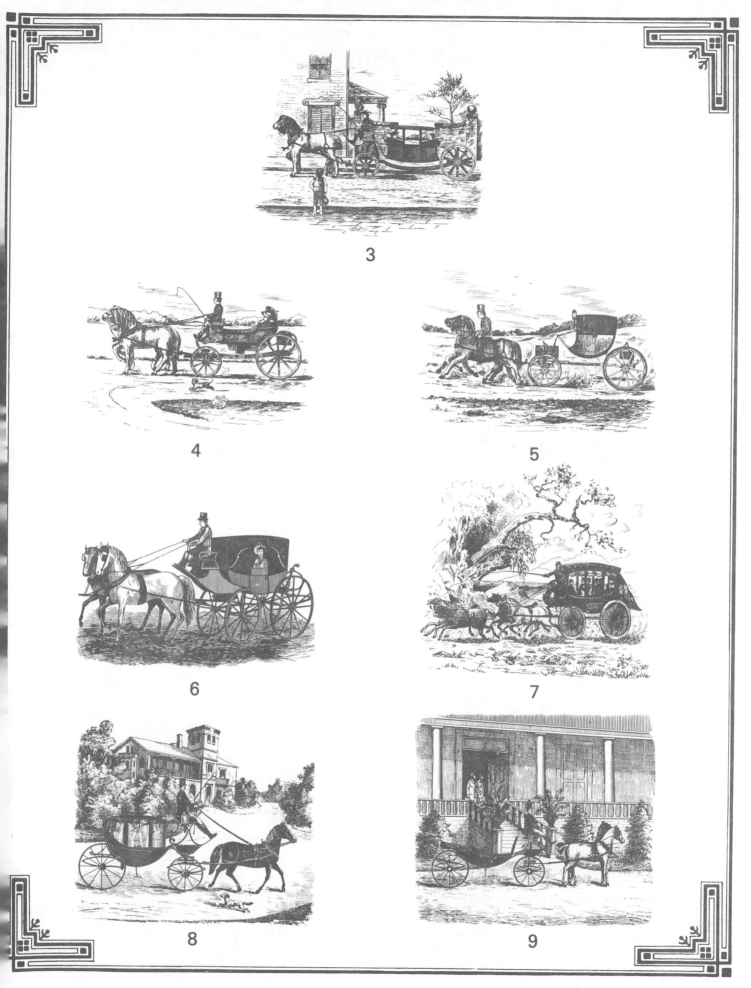

3

4

5

6

7

8

9

HARNESS

THE invention of harness is ascribed to Erichthonius, of Athens.

The use of harness commenced as soon as the horse was trained to draft.

The first horsemen, not being acquainted with the art of governing horses, managed them with a switch, assisted with the accent of the voice.

That shown in the sculptures of Egypt was of a very simple construction. The horses were hitched abreast to a tongue or pole, which was connected to a yoke; this passed over saddles which rested on the withers of the horse.

Solomon had 40,000 stalls for horses and chariots, and plenty of harness.

While the Egyptian yoked his horses to the pole of his chariot, still more primitive customs were adopted in other lands at a later date.

The ancients were well acquainted with the use of the bit. Xenophon, 400 years B. C., describes bits as being in common use in his time in the Grecian States. He speaks of a smooth and sharp kind; the latter, if more severity was required, was to be armed with points or teeth.

In the sculptured equestrian figures of the ancients, something like the branches of a curb are to be found, but in no instance does there appear anything resembling the chain which is necessary to its effect.

The addition of the chain to curb bits is of modern invention. It was used in Italy and France, and was introduced into the English army by proclamation in the reign of Charles I.

"The Spaniards outwitted the French in lining their harness with chains, so that it could not be cut." (Pepys, 1661.)

The French still make use of rope harness, and frequently have nine horses to a diligence, which are driven three abreast.

The single line mode of driving horses, usual on farms and with heavy road teams throughout the west, was made very familiar to many during the late war. The Government six-mule teams are driven by a man riding the near wheel horse, and having a single line to a bridle rein on the near leader. The bit of the off leader is connected by a jockey stick to a hame ring of the near leader, which keeps him in place. The off wheeler is governed by the whip, foot, or occasional touch of his rein. This mode of driving is also practiced in the Netherlands.

Besides the kinds of harness depending upon quality and mounting, other varieties are known by the names of buggy, coach, cart or wagon, according to the vehicle used, and the latter have a division into lead, hip, strap breeching and Yankee, according to the construction and arrangement.

The use of devices for detaching and adjusting harness to horses in the steam fire departments of large cities has become an important factor in the time saved in attending fires.

HARNESS

1. Ancient Pack Saddle.
2. English—16th Century.
3. English—A. D. 1750.
4. Rope.
5. Heavy Draft.
6. Coupe, Single.
7. Beast Collar, Single.
8. U. S. Patent, Overdraw Check—A. D. 1866.
9. U. S. Patent, Suspended—A.D. 1876.

HARNESS

7,999 Establishments in the United States

	1860	1880
Capital Invested, ..	$6,478,184.00	$16,508,079.00
Value of Productions, ...	14,169,037.00	38,081,643.00
Wages Paid, ...	4,150,365.00	7,997,752.00
Hands Employed,..	12,285	21,446

2,543 Patents Granted by the United States

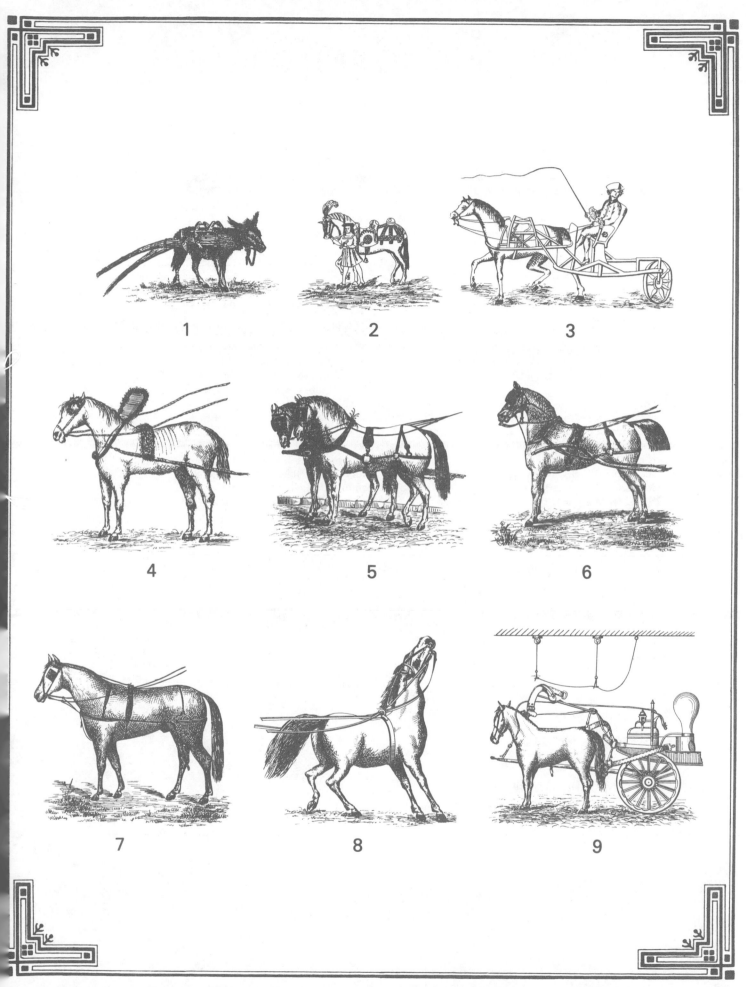

1

2

3

4

5

6

7

8

9

WELL BORING AND DRILLING

JACOB's well, at Sychar, was 9 feet in diameter, 105 feet deep, and was made entirely through solid rock.

The well of Joseph, at Cairo, is the most remarkable work of its kind. It is excavated in the solid rock, with a section 18 x 14 feet, to the depth of 165 feet, where an enlarged chamber is found, in which is cut a reservoir for the water brought up from below. From the front, another shaft, not in the same vertical line with the upper one, is sunk to a further depth of 130 feet, when a bed of gravel is reached, from which the water is obtained. The total depth is 297 feet.

The Chinese mode of boring wells has been practiced in that country from the earliest time. Some of these wells are from 1,500 to 1,800 feet deep, and from five to six inches in diameter.

Artesian wells were first introduced in the province of Artois, France.

The artesian well at Kissengen, Bavaria, was begun in 1832. In 1850 water was reached at a depth of 1,878 feet.

The artesian wells at Chicago, United States, are 700 feet deep, and discharge 1,250,000 gallons daily.

Petroleum in any vast quantity was unknown in the United States until 1845, when oil was obtained while boring for salt near Pittsburgh, Pa.

In August, 1859, operations were commenced at Titusville, Pa., by boring. At the depth of 71 feet, a fountain was reached which yielded about 1,000 gallons daily.

Before the close of the year 1860 the number of borings and wells was estimated to be about 2,000.

In May, 1856, the work of boring wells in the Desert of Sahara was commenced. Water was reached June 19th, and 1,060 gallons per minute were discharged of a temperature of 79 degrees Fah.

Several wells in the United States bored for oil have developed fine flows of mineral water.

One of the most celebrated artesian wells is at Grenelle, near paris, France. It took seven years to complete it. It is 1,802 feet deep. When the water bearing strata were reached, the water was discharged at the rate of 880,000 gallons in twenty-four hours, and the force was so great that water was carried 120 feet above the surface.

The deepest well in the world is said to be near Berlin, Germany. Its depth is 4,170 feet.

The invention of the drive well was made in 1861 by Nelson W. Green, an officer of a New York regiment, during the late civil war. He conceived the idea of driving into the earth small tubes of iron perforated at the bottom, and of attaching a pump at the upper end of the tube. His invention was adopted for the use of the United States army. Its use quickly spread to foreign countries, and it is now an adjunct of the military equipment of all nations, and is common throughout the world.

2,890 petroleum wells were put down in 1883.

WELL BORING AND DRILLING

1. Primitive, Well Drilling.
2. Primitive, Horse Power Drilling.
3. Steam Power Drilling.
4. U. S. Patent, Hand Driving Wells—A. D. 1868.
5. U. S. Patent, Pile Driving Wells—A. D. 1868.
6. U. S. Patent, Rotary Diamond Drilling—A. D. 1881.
7. U. S. Patent, Portable Steam Drilling—A. D. 1884.
8. U. S. Patent, Hydraulic Drilling—A. D. 1884.
9. U. S. Patent, Driven Well System for Cities—A. D. 1884.

WELL BORING AND DRILLING

	Primitive Mode	Present Machine
CAPACITY—		
Feed Drilled per day,	6	50
Hands Employed per day,	2	2

791 Patents Granted by the United States

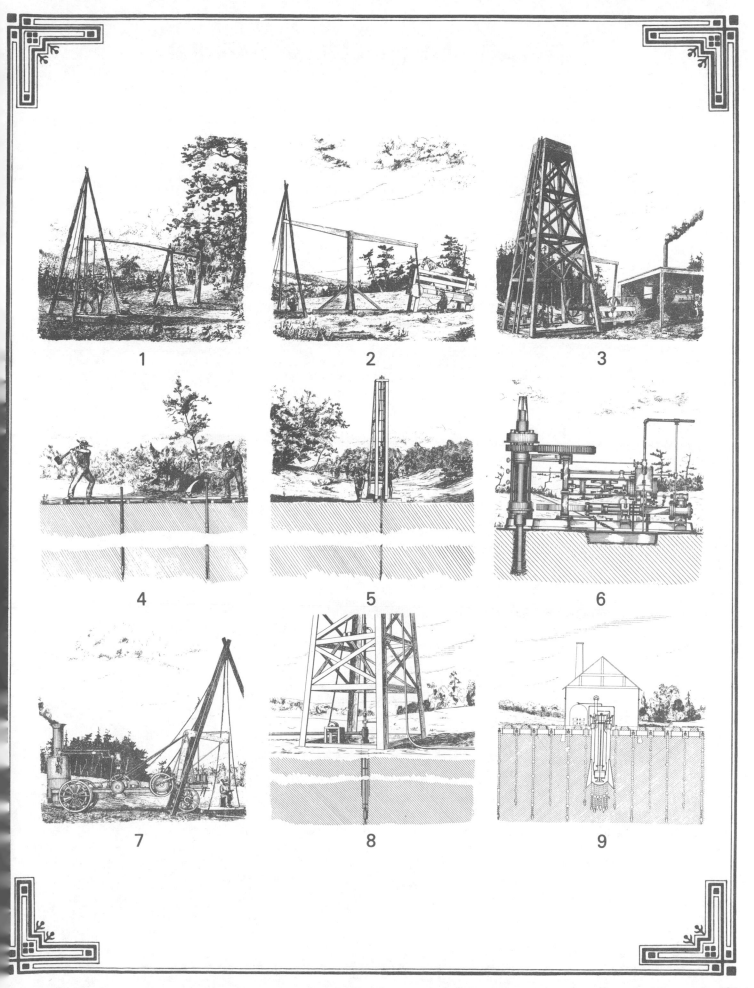

1

2

3

4

5

6

7

8

9

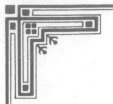

ROAD MAKING MACHINES

THE Carthagenians invented paved roads on a foundation of rough stones consolidated in a mass of mortar, which became solid, making a smooth and lasting road. These roads were built into the most distant provinces for the purpose of facilitating the march of their soldiery and the transportation of supplies. Isidore, a Greek architect of the sixth century, says "the Romans made roads almost over the known world."

Twenty-nine great military roads centered in Rome, which was divided into eleven regions, one hundred and thirteen provinces, and traversed by three hundred and seventy-two great roads, with a length of fifty-two thousand, nine hundred and sixty-four Roman miles.

The first of the great roads was the Appian Way, which was constructed by Appius Claudius Caecus, 331 B. C.: the stones were hewn and closely fitted. Although more than twenty centuries have passed since its construction it is still entire in many places.

During the last African war a paved road was constructed through Spain and Gaul to the Alps. These roads connected the Capital with Savoy, Dauphine, Province of Germany and all parts of Spain, Gaul, Constantinople, Hungary, Macedonia and the mouth of the Danube on the other side of the intervening waters; these roads extended into Sicily, Corsica, Sardinia, England, Asia and Africa. The Roman roads were distinguished by the names Via, Actus, Inter, Semiter, Trames, Callais, etc.

The Via was eight feet wide, and was considered the best.

The Via Militore, near Rome, was double width, or sixteen Roman feet; the middle was paved and divided from the sidewalk by a curb two feet wide and eighteen inches high. The middle was for the infantry and the margin for carriages and equestrians.

ROAD MAKING MACHINES

466 Patents Granted by the United States

The Actus was four feet wide, and was used for single carriages.

The Iter was for horsemen, pack animals and pedestrians, and was three feet wide. The Semiter was eighteen inches wide.

The Callais was a mountain path.

Roman military roads were made with four strata with composite thickness of about three feet. The statumen consisted of two courses of flat stones laid in mortar; the sudus was a rubble of broken stone, mixed with one-third the quantity of quicklime well rammed. The nucleus was a mixture of brick, broken tiles and one-third the quantity of lime or gravel, and the stated proportion of lime laid on while hot from slacking.

In Persia the royal roads ran beside the common roads, and were used only by the King; they were kept in much better order than other roads, and were called "the King's highway."

The Moguls constructed roads in India with "distance stones" at the end of every Koss.

The Grand Trunk road connecting Calcutta with Peshawur on the borders of Afghanistan was built by the British.

The Roman roads of England were built in the second, third and fourth centuries, criminals and Roman soldiery being employed thereon. The four principals were from Kent, via London, to Cardigan Bay in Wales; from St. Davids, Wales, via Birmingham, Derby and York, to Tynemouth; from Cornwall to Lincoln, and from St. Davids to Southampton. The Britons neglected the roads built by the Romans. The English government made little attempt to improve the roads till the reign of Charles II.

Highways were first made public in England by the Romans. Edward I ordered the roads widened and cleared of trees within two hundred feet of the road to prevent robberies.

The road built by Napoleon, from Geneva to Milan, cost the French Government three million, two hundred and fifty thousand dollars.

"Macadamized roads," are named from the inventor, MacAdam, who used small, angular broken stone of a hard variety. He was made Surveyor General of the roads of Bristol.

The National road of the United States, from Baltimore across the Alleghanies, extends six hundred and fifty and five-eighths miles, and is macadamized for thirty feet of its width.

ROAD MAKING MACHINES

1. Primitive Leveller.
2. Primitive Carrying Scraper.
3. U. S. Patent, Sulky Scraper—A.D. 1831.
4. U. S. Patent, Wheel Scraper—A. D. 1839.
5. U. S. Patent, Drag Scraper—A.D. 1850.
6. U. S. Patent, Self-Loading Cart—A. D. 1850.
7. U. S. Patent, Self-Loading Cart—A. D. 1867.
8. U. S. Patent, Revolving Scraper—A. D. 1879.
9. U. S. Patent, Self-Loading Cart—A. D. 1881.
10. U. S. Patent, Road Builder—A. D. 1883.
11. U. S. Patent, Wheel Scraper—A. D. 1884.

1

2

3

4

5

6

7

8

9

10

11

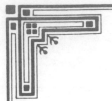

SWEEPING

THE word besom, meaning broom, is used by Isaiah in speaking of the destruction of Babylon, "I will sweep it with the besom of destruction."

Brooms having long sticks to them were used by the Romans; they had also bristle brushes.

In Paris, in 1285, an order was issued that each citizen should keep the street clean in front of his own house.

In 1750, Benjamin Atkman, of Bradford Co., Pa., commenced the manufacture of brooms from broom corn. A few years after he took B. Croasdale into partnership, and they jointly held the trade in brooms until 1816, supplying the markets of Philadelphia, Baltimore, Trenton and New York.

The street sweeping machines of Paris have a broom attached to the rear of a two-wheeled vehicle by means of a frame work, which is so hinged to the axle of the vehicle as to enable the conductor on the box in front to raise it out of contact with the pavement or to depress it for service at pleasure.

Nearly all the bristles used in making brushes in the United States are imported from Russia. They come assorted as to length and stiffness.

The improvement in breeding the American hog has nearly deprived him of usefulness as a bristle producer.

Horse hair, Tampico grass and steel and brass are also extensively used in the manufacture of brooms.

There are brooms in England called heath brooms, which are made of a small shrub growing on the sandy heaths of Great Britain. A similar shrub is found in great abundance in Spain, and is doubtless the same which Pliny speaks of as covering the mountains near Carthagena. This shrub is called "broom," and is supposed to have given the name to implements, for sweeping.

The material of which brooms are generally made is a kind of Sorghum called broom corn, which is extensively cultivated in Europe and America.

Very simple machinery is used in the manufacture of brooms, consisting of a wooden roller, turned by a crank for the purpose of winding on the cord. One hand holds the broom handle, and, while winding on the twine, the brush is supplied with the other. The machine has also a bench and a rag wheel to hold the cord when wound on the roller.

The societies of Shakers in the United States are largely engaged in making brooms.

SWEEPING

1. Primitive, Hand Broom.
2. Primitive Street Sweeping.
3. French Street Sweeping—A. D. 1836.
4. U. S. Patent, Hand Broom—A. D. 1852.
5. U. S. Patent, Hand Sweeper—A. D. 1858.
6. U. S. Patent, Hand Broom—A. D. 1852.
7. U. S. Patent, Hand Sweeper—A. D. 1884.
8. U. S. Patent, Street Sweeper—A. D. 1884.

SWEEPING

CAPACITY—	Primitive Mode	Present Machine
Street Sweepers		
Miles per day, ...	1	15
Hands Employed		
per day, ...	1	1

123 Patents Granted by the United States

1

2

3

4

5

6

7

8

ROAD ENGINES

MURDOCK, a Scotch engineer, about 1786 constructed a small locomotive, which ran on the high road near Redruth, Scotland.

Symington, of Scotland, and Oliver Evans, of America, also constructed models designed for the same purpose.

One of the earlier forms of traction engines was Boydell's. This had endless chains of boards fitted to its wheels, forming a sort of endless railway, which was laid down and taken up by the engine as it proceeded.

The success of railways, and the difficulties attending the use of locomotives on ordinary roads, caused a cessation of efforts toward the improvement of road engines until about the year 1856, when the subject was revived with a view to the adaptation of such engines to agricultural purposes. Of late years several varieties have been constructed which fulfill their intended purpose with considerable success.

A traction engine for running on ice has been employed for carrying passengers between St. Petersburg and Cronstadt, in Russia.

ROAD ENGINES

1. U. S. Patent, Steam Wagon—A. D. 1817.
2. U. S. Patent, Traction Engine—A. D. 1873.
3. U. S. Patent, Power Steering Road Engine—A. D. 1881.
4. U. S. Patent, Road and Agricultural Engine— A. D. 1882.
5. U. S. Patent, Adjustable Leveling Road Engine— A. D. 1883.
6. U. S. Patent, Winding Drum Road Engine—A. D. 1884.

ROAD ENGINES

469 Patents Granted by the United States

1

2

3

4

5

6

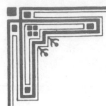

STEAM ENGINES

BAPTISTA Porta, in 1600, contrived an apparatus for exhibiting the power of steam.

Solomon De Caus, about 1620, wrote a book in which he claims to have invented a steam engine.

The first engine on this Continent was brought over from England in 1736; and prior to the Revolutionary war there were but two steam engines in the Colonies; one was built for use in a distillery in Philadelphia, and the other was imported, as stated above, for the Schuyler Copper Mines, in Passaic, N. J. Both were of the Newcomen type.

James Watt, of Glasgow, when repairing a model of a Newcomen engine in 1763, began a series of improvements which finally rendered the steam engine universally applicable. To avoid losses of heat in the steam cylinder, he attached in 1765 the separate condenser, thus saving three-fourths of the injection water needed in the Newcomen engine.

The first steam engine constructed in this country was built at Philadelphia, Pa. in 1779.

Oliver Evans, of Philadelphia, Pa., invented the "high pressure non-condensing steam engine."

In 1785 Mr. Evans first applied steam to the grinding of plaster and the sawing of stone, and to flour mills.

A recent writer has calculated that the engines of a first-class Atlantic steamer contain 6,000 parts, with 2,270 boiler tubes, 4,456 condenser tubes, 64,888 rivets, 10,407 nuts, 3,000 studs, 7,868 bolts, 1,582 boiler stays, 1,356 furnace bars, and 1,144 pins. In addition to these there are 100 moving parts, 271 steam pipes, 147 valves, 37 levers, 24 furnaces, and 172 pieces belonging to the pumping-out arrangements. The number of auxiliary engines would be about 23.

An idea of the extreme lightness of steam may be obtained by the statement that it takes 27.2222 cubic feet of steam at the pressure of one atmosphere to weigh one pound, avoirdupois.

Some conception of the enormous results of steam power may be gained from the fact that the aggregate steam power in use in the world is at present three and one-half millions horse-power employed in stationary engines, and ten millions horse-power in locomotive engines. This force is maintained without the consumption of animal food, except by the miners who dig the coal, and the force maintained in their muscles is to the force generated by the product of their labor about 1 to 1,080. This steam power is equal to the working force of twenty-five million of horses, and one horse consumes three times as much food as one man. The steam power, therefore, is equivalent to the saving of food for seventy-five millions of human beings.

Further, three power looms attended by one man produce seventy-eight pieces of cotton fabric, against four pieces produced by one hand loom worked by one man in the year 1800.

A carpenter's planing machine does the work of twenty men.

STEAM ENGINES

1. First Steam Engine—B. C. 200.
2. Piston Steam Engine—A. D. 1690.
3. U. S. Patent, Beam Engine—A. D. 1849.
4. U. S. Patent, Beam Engine—A. D. 1876.
5. U. S. Patent, Direct Acting Engine—A. D. 1882.
6. U. S. Patent, Horizontal Engine—A. D. 1883.
7. U. S. Patent, Duplex Engine—A. D. 1883.

1

STEAM ENGINES

4,337 Patents Granted by the United States

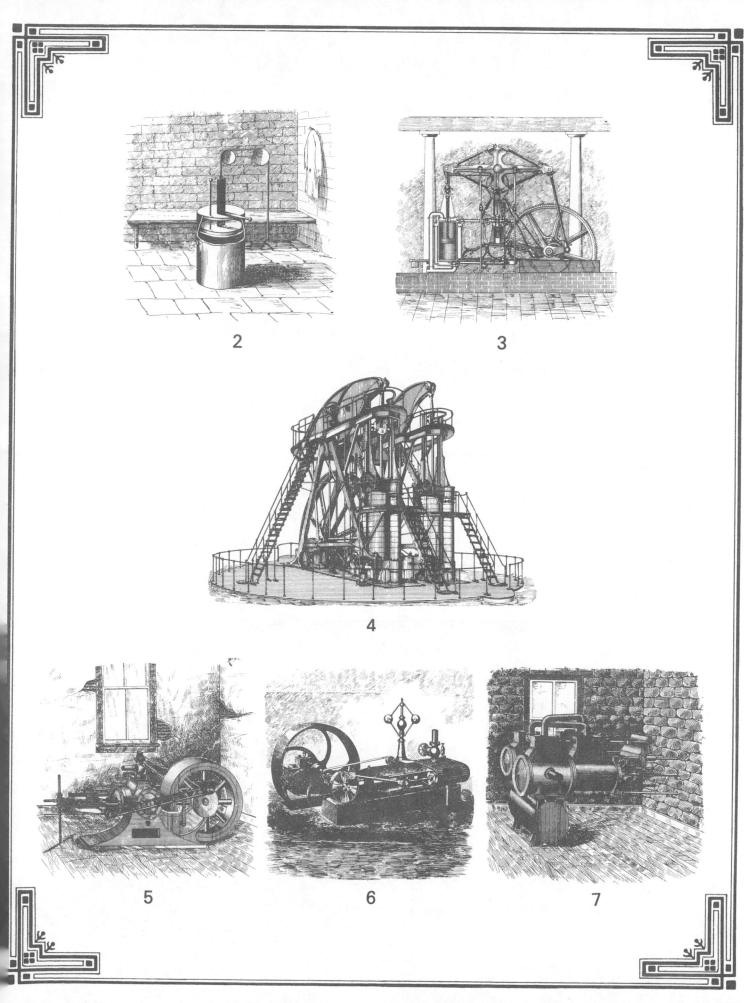

2

3

4

5

6

7

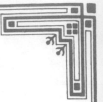

STEAM ENGINES, ROTARY AND OSCILLATING

THE original steam engine was the AEolipile, exhibited in Alexandria, Egypt, 150 B. C. It was a rotary steam engine, the principle being the same as that of the modern turbine water wheel.

Hero, who derived much information from Archimedes, described three modes in which steam could be used as a mechanical power: 1st, to raise water by its elasticity; 2nd, to elevate a weight by its expansive power; and 3d, to produce a rotary motion by its reaction on the atmosphere.

Nerbrest, in his Astronomia Europæa, in 1680, speaks of drawing a car by an æolipile, which ejected the steam upon wings whose axes were geared to the wheels of the car.

The oscillatory cylinder engine was patented in England in 1813.

In a rotary engine the piston is attached to a shaft, and revolves with it within a cylinder, the axis of which is parallel with the axis of rotation of the piston or vane.

Oscillating engines have their piston rods attached directly to the crank pin, and as the crank revolves the cylinder oscillates upon trunnions, one on each side of it, through which the steam enters and leaves the steam chest. The valves are within the steam chest, oscillating with the cylinder.

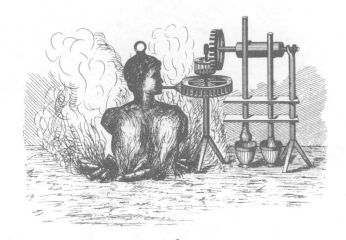

1

2

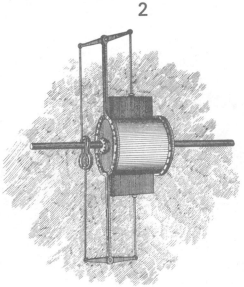

3

STEAM ENGINES— ROTARY AND OSCILLATING

921 Patents Granted by the United States

STEAM ENGINES— ROTARY & OSCILLATING

1. Rotary Steam Jet—A. D. 1629.
2. Rotary Steam Pressure—A. D. 1769.
3. U. S. Patent, Rotary Steam Pressure—A.D. 1816.
4. U. S. Patent, Oscillating—A. D. 1827.
5. U. S. Patent, Oscillating—A. D. 1832.
6. U.S. Patent, Reaction Steam Jet—A.D. 1834.
7. U. S. Patent, Steam Jet—A. D. 1845.
8. U. S. Patent, Compound Direct Acting—A. D. 1869.
9. U. S. Patent, Rotary Steam Pressure—A. D. 1882.

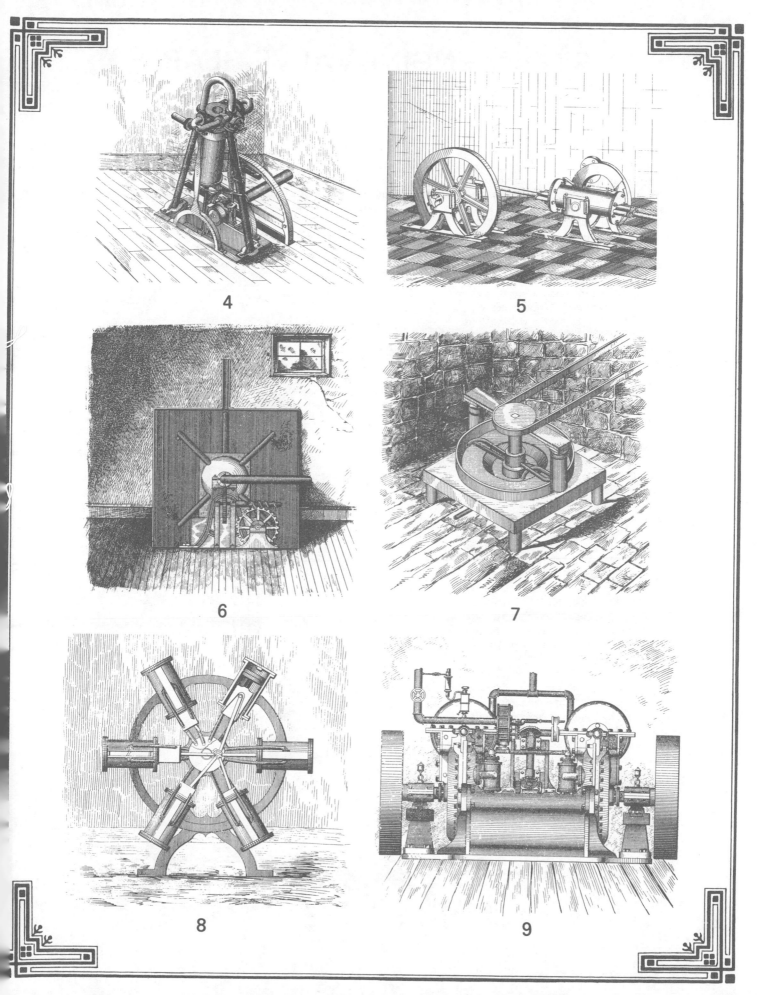

4

5

6

7

8

9

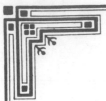

STEAM ENGINE VALVE GEAR

THE first means of shutting and opening the passages of steam engines were cocks, and as these were all worked by hand the closest and most constant attention was required.

Dr. Papin invented the piston and lever safety valve in 1710.

In 1711 Messrs. Newcomen & Cawley contracted to build a steam engine that would operate pumps for draining a coalery at Griff, Warwickshire, England.

When this engine was on trial the builders were surprised to see it make "several strokes very quick together," when, after a search for the cause of this action, they found a hole in the piston, which let cold water into the cylinder and condensed the steam, whereas, before this, the steam in the cylinder had been condensed by the application of cold water to the outside.

This circumstance led to the application of a jet of water into the cylinder. In order to cause this jet of water to enter the cylinder at the right time, which was at the completion of the stroke of the piston, a float was so arranged in a pipe at the side of the cylinder that when the steam was strong it would rise and open the injection valve. This was a self-actuated valve gear, but with it only from six to ten strokes of the piston per minute could be attained.

Finally, Humphrey Potter, a boy who attended the engine, in 1713, added what he called a "scoggan," which was a catch that the beam always opened so that the piston could make as high as sixteen strokes per minute.

This device was used for several years, but "being perplexed with catches and strings, Mr. Henry Beighton, in an engine he had built at Newcastle-upon-Tyne, in 1718, took them all away but the beam itself, and supplied them in a much better manner."

Watt introduced the rotary ball governor, throttle valve, steam gage, indicator and register.

STEAM ENGINE VALVE GEAR

679 Patents Granted by the United States

The detachable, adjustable, or drop cut-off valve gear was patented by Frederick E. Sickels, of New York City, in 1842.

The application of the governor to determine the point of cut-off was made by Zackariah Allen and George Corliss, of Rhode Island, in 1849.

The valve gear is the system of valves and of actuating mechanism which distribute the steam as the engine passes through its cycle of motion.

STEAM ENGINE VALVE GEAR

1. Automatic—A. D. 1717.
2. Eccentric—A. D. 1785.
3. English Shifting Cam—A. D. 1802.
4. English Hand Shifting Eccentric—A.D. 1834.
5. U. S. Patent, Fly Wheel Governor—A. D. 1839.
6. U. S. Patent, Link Motion—A. D. 1842.
7. U. S. Patent, Valve Gear—A. D. 1849.
8. U. S. Patent, Link Shifted by Steam—A. D. 1867.
9. U. S. Patent, Electric Generator Engine—A. D. 1883.

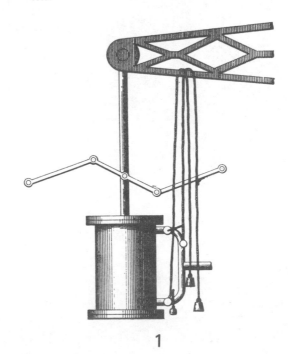

1

2

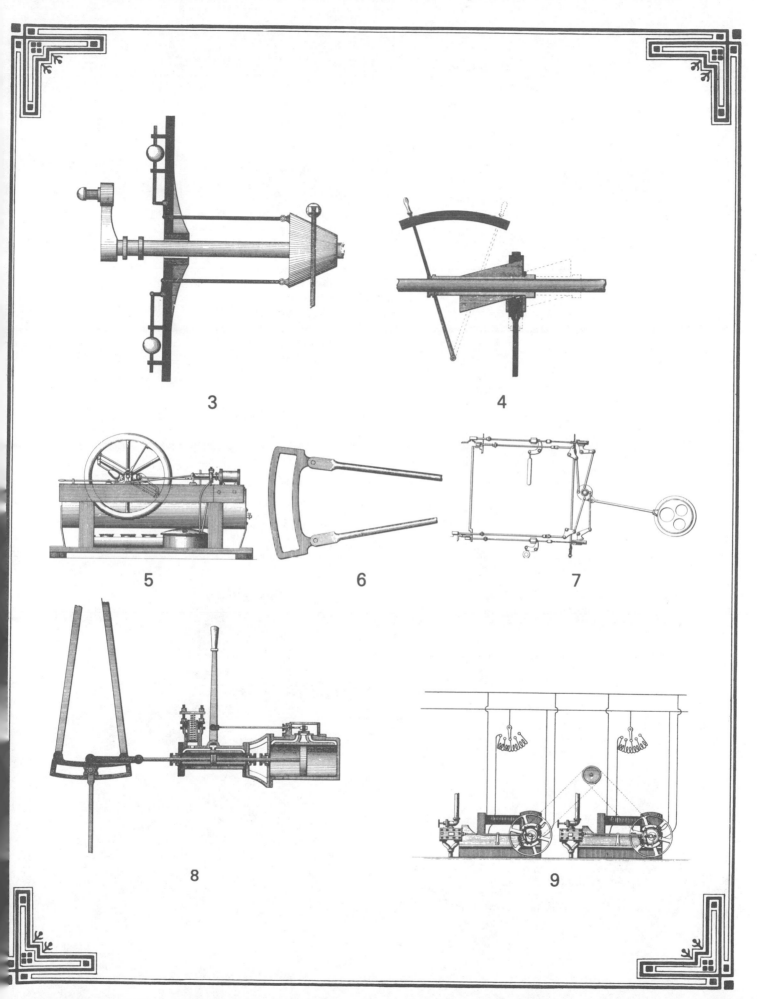

3

4

5

6

7

8

9

STEAM PUMPING ENGINES

THE Marquis of Worcester, in his "Hundred Inventions," published in 1663, mentions a number of experiments which he made of the expansive power of steam, and claims that his attention was directed to this subject by an incident which occurred while he was a prisoner in the Tower of London. He had ben preparing some food over a fire when the cover of the vessel was suddenly driven with great violence up the chimney. While this story is probably apocryphal, it is believed that the Marquis invented an engine which he thought could be made conducive to the public interests in raising water from pits or wells, and this engine was afterwards recommended to Louis XIV by Sir Samuel Morland for the purpose of irrigating the grounds at St. Germain. The Marquis is claimed as the inventor who discovered a mode of applying steam as a mechanical agent, and he secured the passage by Parliament of an act to enable his heirs for ninety-nine years to receive the sole benefit, profit and advantage from, as he termed it, his "water commanding engine."

This engine was, however, incomplete and crude.

In 1698, Captain Savary obtained a patent for a new method of clearing coal and other mines of water, and he may be justly considered as the first person who rendered steam applicable to manufacturing purposes.

Savary's engine was employed with good results in the drainage of mines in Cornwall and Devonshire, England.

The engines of the Marquis of Worcester, Savary, Papin and Newcomen, were all pumping engines.

Oliver Evans, of Philadelphia, was one of the first, if not the first inventor, to apply the high pressure principle to the steam engine, and he succeeded in introducing it into quite general use in this country before his death. In the year 1817, he constructed a pumping engine for the Fairmount Water Works, the boilers for which were worked at a pressure of 200 pounds to the square inch, but after two explosions the engine was abandoned and water wheels introduced.

The largest stationary engine in the world is at the famous zinc mines at Friedensville, Pa. It is known as "The President," and it is said that there is no pumping engine in the world that can compare with it. Its regular work is to raise 17,500 gallons of water every minute, and it has raised as high as 19,000 gallons in a minute, from a depth of 350 feet. The driving wheels are 35 feet in diameter, and weigh 40 tons each. The sweep rod is 40 feet long, the cylinder 110 inches in diameter, and the piston rod 18 inches in diameter, with a 10-foot stroke.

STEAM PUMPING ENGINES

1. Single Acting Pumping Engine—A. D. 1774.
2. U. S. Patent, Double Plunger Mining Pump—A.D. 1870.
3. U. S. Patent, Duplex Pumping Engine—A. D. 1875.
4. U. S. Patent, Double End Steam Pump—A. D. 1876.
5. U. S. Patent, Steam Pumping Engine—A. D. 1881.
6. U. S. Patent, Gas Motor Applied to Pumping—A. D. 1883.
7. U. S. Patent, Compound Pumping Engine—A. D. 1883.

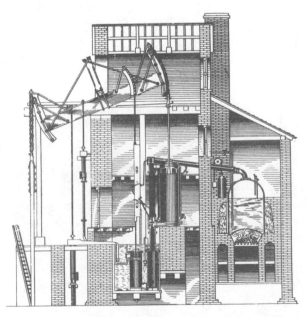

1

STEAM PUMPING ENGINES

217 Patents Granted by the United States

2

3

4

5

6

7

STEAM AND AIR BRAKES

CAR brakes, until the advent of the atmospheric brake, were actuated by a winding drum connecting with chains and levers, the power of the brakeman being applied to a hand-wheel on the car platform.

The Westinghouse atmospheric brake has been adopted on most of the railway lines in the United States and Europe.

Its chief features are, first, the use of compressed atmospheric air as a means of applying the brakes; and, second, putting the whole braking apparatus under the direct control of the locomotive engineer, so that he can apply the brakes at pleasure, instantaneously or gradually, and with any desired power, limited only by the power of the air-compressing apparatus and the strength of the air vessels.

At a test of the Westinghouse air brake on the Kansas Pacific Railway May 12, 1871, a train going at the rate of 45 miles an hour was stopped within a distance of 250 feet.

At a recent test of the Westinghouse air brake, a freight train of fifty cars, 1,900 feet long, and weighing 2,000,000 pounds, drawn by a heavy engine, was brought to a standstill in 12¼ seconds, and within 200 feet from the marking post, the train running at the rate of 20 miles an hour.

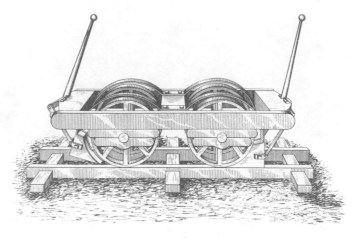

1

STEAM AND AIR BRAKES

290 Patents Granted by the United States

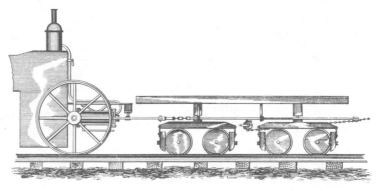

2

STEAM AND AIR BRAKES

1. U. S. Patent, Hand Power—A. D. 1840.
2. U. S. Patent, Steam—A. D. 1858.
3. U. S. Patent, Air—A. D. 1860.
4. U. S. Patent, Steam—A. D. 1862.
5. U. S. Patent, Locomotive Drive Wheel—A. D. 1874.
6. U. S. Patent, Vaccum—A.D. 1875.

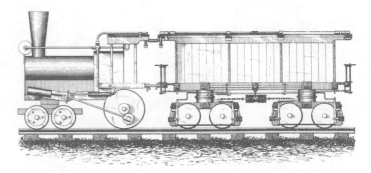

3

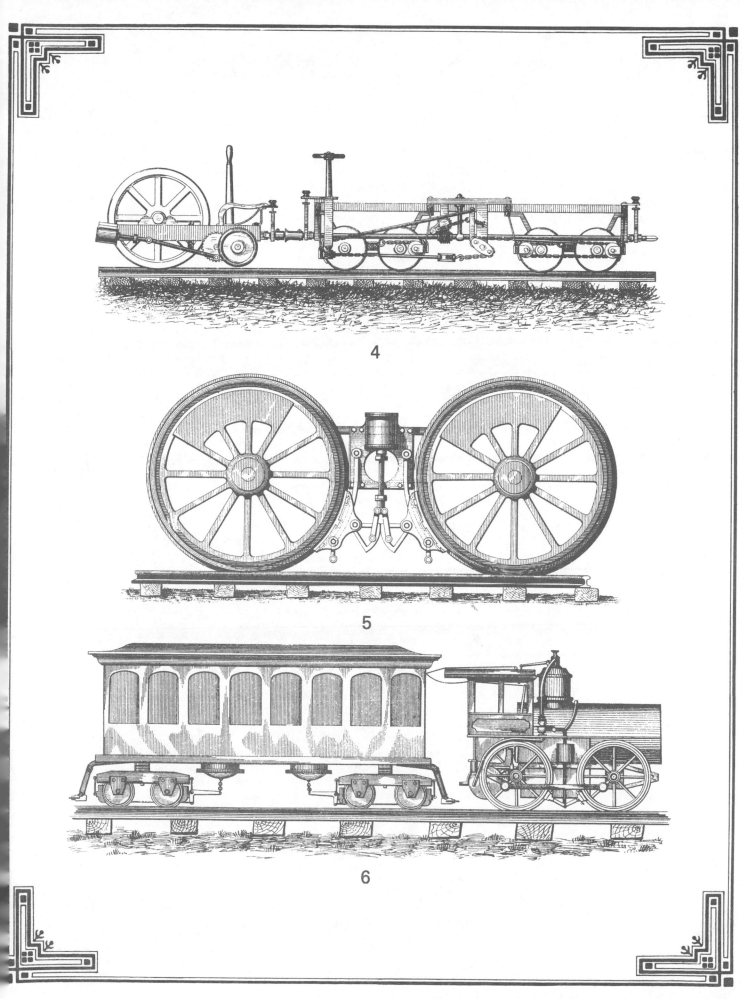

4

5

6

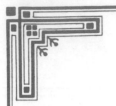

AIR AND GAS ENGINES

FOR more than a century the attention of mechanicians has been directed to means for making air and gas available in driving machinery.

Amonton, France, in 1699, had an atmospheric firewheel, or air engine, in which a heated column of air was made to drive a wheel. Some have attempted to make available the expansion of air, previously mechanically condensed and stored in reservoirs. It was not understood, apparently, that the valuable effect would only be equal to the force employed in condensing the air, minus friction, leakage and other incidentals. This form settled down to two classes of machines—

1st. Those which were locomotives, as in Bouepas's air-driven carriage, patented in 1828, where the air was condensed in tanks and admitted to the alternate ends of a cylinder, which had a reciprocating piston, connected in the usual manner to the crank and driveshaft. Von Rathen used the same device in 1848, at Putney, England, where he ran an air locomotive at the rate of ten or twelve miles an hour.

2nd. Those in which a body of air is condensed into a reservoir, placed at the bottom of a shaft, or in a situation where the prime motor cannot be set up. In this case the engine in the mine is run by the air from the reservoir during a lull in the force of the prime motor.

Medhurst secured patent on this in England, in 1799. He condensed air to one-fifteenth of its volume, and stored it for this purpose. Fisk's U. S. patent air reservoir in 1865 had a similar purpose.

Another form of air engine has two chambers filled with air or gas, connected by pipes with the respective ends of a cylinder, in which a piston reciprocates as the bodies of air in the cylinders are alternately expanded and contracted. Sterling's English patent, 1827, was of this character, and is stated by Chambers "to have been unsuccessful, owing to mechanical defects, and to the unforseen accumulation of heat not fully extracted by the sieves or small passages in the cool part of the regenerator, of which

the external surface was not sufficiently large to throw off the uncovered heat when the engine was working with highly compressed air."

Sterling is said to have been the originator, in 1816, of the regenerator wherein the heat of the exhausting air is made to heat surfaces which communicate heat to the incoming air for the next charge. The same idea was found in the English patent of Glazebrook, in 1797.

Sterling made improvements in 1840, which he also patented. In this engine two strong, air-tight vessels are connected with opposite ends of a cylinder, in which a piston works in the usual manner; four-fifths of the interior space in these vessels are occupied by two similar air vessels, or plungers, suspended to the opposite extremities of a beam, and capable of being alternately moved up and down to the extent of the remaining fifth. By the motion of these interior vessels the air to be operated upon is moved from one end of the exterior vessel to the other, and as one end is kept at a high temperature, and the other as cold as possible, when the air is brought to the hot end it becomes heated and has its pressure increased, whereas its heat and pressure are diminished when it is forced to the cold end. Now, as the interior vessels move in opposite directions, it follows that the pressure of the enclosed air in the one vessel is increased, while that of the other is diminished; a difference of pressure is produced on opposite sides of the piston which is made to move from one end of the cylinder to the other; the piston is connected with a fly-wheel, and motion communicated in the usual way. In this engine the air received heat at the temperature of 650° Fah, and discharged the last heat at 150° Fah. The efficiency of a perfect engine with those limits of temperature would be 0.45 and its consumption of coal 0.73 of a pound per horse power per hour. The actual consumption of coal per horse power per hour was about two and two-tenths pounds, being three times the consumption of a theoretically perfect engine, and corresponding to an actual efficiency of 0.15, or one-third of the maximum theoretical efficiency.

Sterling's air engine was more economical than the double-action steam engine.

A third form of the apparatus embraces but few features. These have been modified by independent inventors to such an extent that they now represent more than eighty patents. Glazebrook seems to have fully anticipated the usefulness and the future of the air engine. His second patent in 1801 has a refrigerator whose use is not to cool the pump wherein the air is condensed, but to deprive the escaping gas of its heat, in case a gas be used of so expansive a character as to preclude its being ejected into the atmosphere after using. He cites carbonic acid and other gases and compounds. He only antedated the engine of Brunel by three years, which was intended to be used without the escape of carbonic acid.

Lillie's air engine, patented in 1819, is in the same line of invention; the air is compressed by mechanical force, passed through heated tubes, expanded against a piston and there escapes into the open air. Air engines are used extensively for driving light machinery, and are very desirable where water is scarce.

The claim for the Ericsson engine was that he intended to use the same power, over and over again, by the means of a regenerator. The regenerator was used by Sterling in 1816, and Glazebrook in 1797, in air engines.

The principle on which the Ericsson regenerator rests is the repeated use of the same caloric. In 1852 a ship was built, one thousand tons burden, two hundred and fifty feet long, with paddle wheels thirty-two feet in diameter, to be propelled by air. On January 4th, 1853, the ship on her trial trip made twelve knots an hour, with the wind, using only six tons of fuel per day.

On the second trial the greatest speed attained was nine knots. The ship, named after the inventor, failed to establish the validity of the principle involved. He took out another patent in 1855 for certain novelties in the apparatus. Ericsson patented improvements in air engines in 1851, 1855, 1856, 1858 and 1860.

The first gas engines were gunpowder engines; the gas generated by the explosion being the means of expelling the air, the condensation of the gases producing a partial vacuum in the chamber.

D. Hautefeuille, in 1678, first used this power.

Hughens applied it in a cylinder so that the atmospheric pressure might force a piston downward when the vacuum was thus formed beneath it. In 1791 Barber obtained an English patent for a gas engine, in which a stream of carbureted hydrogen gas was introduced at one induction port and a quantity of atmospheric air at the other, the resulting combustion giving an explosive force against the piston.

Street, in 1794, proposed to use the expansive power of heated gas instead of its explosive power. Lebon's French patent of 1799 described the distillation of carbureted hydrogen from coal, and its introduction into the cylinder beneath the piston, and, simultaneously at another channel, a proper proportion of atmospheric air. The mixed gases were exploded by the electric spark, their dilation furnishing the desired motive power.

Brunel's gas engine, in 1825, consisted of five distinct cylindrical vessels. Davy and Faraday, in 1823, succeeded in reducing several gases to a liquid state by means of great pressure and very low temperature. This discovery again turned attention to gas engines. Cooper, in 1835, described an engine in which one part oxygen and two parts hydrogen were

ignited to produce a vacuum alternately on each side of a piston. Johnson's patent of 1841, proposed to introduce pure hydrogen gas and oxygen, instead of atmospheric air. The Otto and Langens gas engine is an upright hollow column having a heavy piston, whose rod is a rack acting upon cog-wheels on the fly-wheel shaft; as the piston ascends the cog-wheel slips loosely on the shaft, and the mixed gases, coal gas and air are exploded by communication with the gas jet, which is kept constantly burning.

As the gases rapidly condense after explosion the atmospheric pressure, aided by the weight of the piston, is made effective upon the shaft of the wheel by the engagement of the rack teeth with those of the spur wheel.

In Lenoir's gas engine, now much employed in France, the source of power is the expansion arising from the explosion of gas. Air and gas are admitted to a cylinder in the proportion II to I; a spark from a galvanic battery is sent through it; the spark explodes the mixture, and the expansion consequent on this explosion drives a piston to the other end of the cylinder. Mechanism does all the rest; opens a slide valve to permit exit to the exploded mixture, drives the piston back by the momentum of a fly-wheel, opens tubes for the admission of new air and gas, establishes

connection again with the battery, and prepares for a renewal of the action, and so on continuously. These engines are costly in the first instance, and many precautions are necessary to prevent them being overheated; but they require no fireman, and are rather cheaper to work than steam engines; consequently they are much employed for two to four-horse power purposes.

AIR AND GAS ENGINES

403 Patents Granted by the United States

AIR AND GAS ENGINES

1. Gunpowder Engine—A.D. 1680.
2. Primitive, Air Engine—A. D. 1794.
3. U. S. Patent, Hot Air Engine—A. D. 1827.
4. U. S. Patent, Explosive Gas Engine—A.D. 1838.
5. U. S. Patent, Explosive Gas Engine—A. D. 1844.
6. U. S. Patent, Explosive Gas Engine—A.D. 1867.
7. U. S. Patent, Bi-sulphide of Carbon Engine—A. D. 1882.
8. U. S. Patent, Steam and Hot Air Engine—A. D. 1883.
9. U. S. Patent, Explosive Gas Engine—A.D. 1883.
10. U. S. Patent, Explosive Gas Engine—A.D. 1883.
11. U. S. Patent, Explosive Gas Engine—A.D. 1883.
12. U. S. Patent, Explosive Gas Engine—A. D. 1884.

1

2

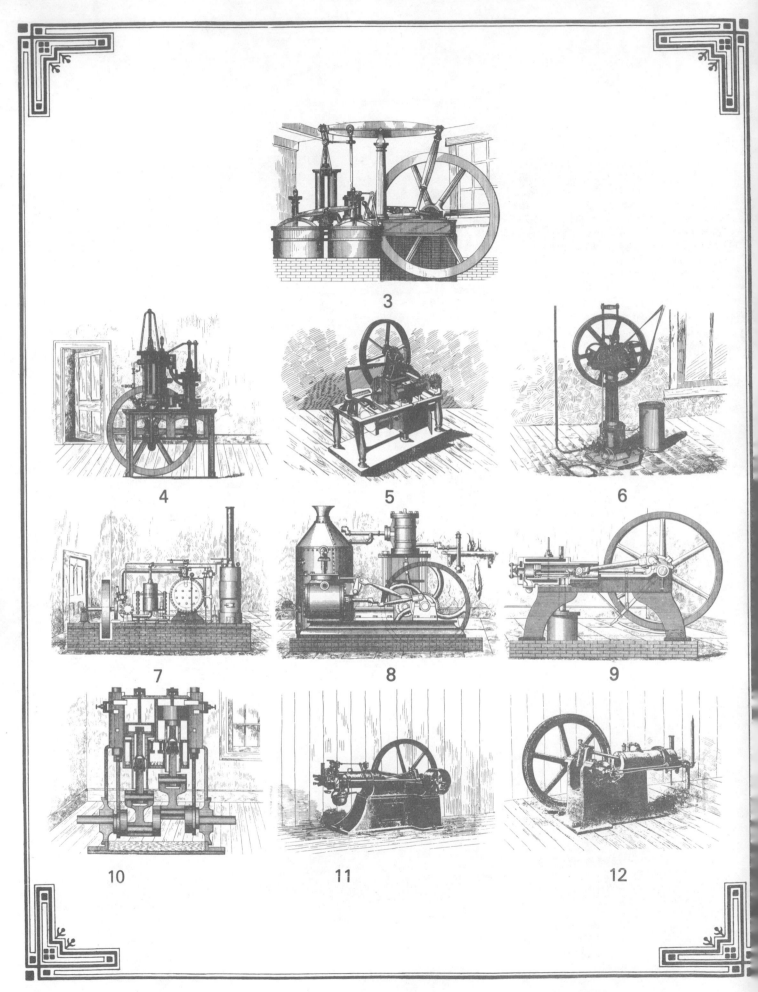

3

4

5

6

7

8

9

10

11

12